What a
Difference a
Daddy
Makes

What a Difference a Daddy Makes

The Indelible Imprint a Dad Leaves on His Daughter's Life

Dr. Kevin Leman

A JANET THOMA BOOK

THOMAS NELSON PUBLISHERS
Nashville

Published in Nashville, Tennessee, by Thomas Nelson, Inc.

Scripture quotations are from THE NEW KING JAMES VERSION. Copyright © 1979, 1980, 1982, Thomas Nelson, Inc., Publishers.

Library of Congress Cataloging-in-Publication Data

Leman, Kevin.
    What a difference a daddy makes / Kevin Leman.
      p. cm.
    Includes bibliographical references.
    ISBN 0-8407-3449-2
    1. Fathers and daughters. 2. Parenting—United States. 3. Fathers and daughters—Religious aspects—Christianity. I. Title.

HQ755.85.L447 2000
306.874'2—dc21

                                      99-022184
                                         CIP

Printed in the United States of America
1 2 3 4 5 6 BVG 05 04 03 02 01 00

Dedication

This book is affectionately dedicated to my four daughters—Holly Kristine Leman, Kristin Leman O'Reilly, Hannah Elizabeth Leman, and Lauren Beth Leman. It is a privilege, an awesome responsibility, and a great joy to be your dad. What a difference each of you has made in my life!

It is also dedicated to my son, Kevin Anderson Leman II, an awesome artist who has such a creative sense of humor. Kevin, you are great . . . and someday you will be famous! My wish and prayer for you is that someday you'll have the privilege of being a dad. You'll be a great one.

I love you all very much!

Contents

Section One
The Daddy Difference

CHAPTER 1
The Missing Ingredient

"Please, please, please, please, *please,*" Shirli Hunt practically prayed. "Don't sing anything patriotic."

Unfortunately, that's exactly what the teacher was planning to do.

The year was 1935. A new wave of Americanism was spreading across the land, and, like so many people in that moment in history, Shirli Hunt's father was passionately patriotic.

"Shirli, you should be very proud to be an American," her father told her.

Shortly before World War II, a pro-Hitler German had walked into a barber shop Shirli's dad frequented and started praising the Third Reich. Shirli's dad leapt out of the barber chair—shaving cream still covering half of his face—and pushed the man up against the wall. "If you don't believe in America, you can leave," he half shouted, "but you're not going to stand here and talk against this country."

Whenever a song was played—on the wireless or at public outings—and America was even *mentioned,* Shirli's father insisted that the entire Wingham family stand to show their respect. They could be in the middle of dinner with guests, but if a song came on the radio in the background

("In those days, people had the radio going all the time," Shirli remembers), Shirli's entire family pushed back their chairs and stood.

That's what led to Shirli's desperate plea. At the time, she was attending middle school, and her teacher was leading the class in several folk songs: "I've Been Working on the Railroad," "Flow Gently, Sweet Afton," and "Oh! Susanna."

So far, so good.

Then the teacher announced, "Let's sing 'America, the Beautiful.'"

Shirli felt like she was going to melt in her seat.

"I sat for one stanza thinking, *I don't have to get up because my dad isn't here; he'll never know.*"

After all, she was sitting in the front row. Everybody could see her, and the last thing a thirteen-year-old girl wants is to be embarrassed.

But the pressure became too great. Shirli could see her father's face, and she could hear his forceful words: *When you walk out that door, you walk out representing the Wingham family, and don't you forget it!*

Suddenly, a room full of seventh graders paled in comparison to the shadow of that forceful, loving man. As the class broke into the second stanza, Shirli rose on weak knees and wobbled to her feet. She just couldn't help herself.

After the song, Shirli's actions created a bit of discussion. One of the boys argued with the teacher, "Shirli didn't have to stand. We weren't singing 'The Star-Spangled Banner.'"

"Oh yes, I did have to stand," Shirli shot right back. "You don't know my father."

Sixty years later, Shirli's eyes still glisten as she looks back on that incident and explains, "My relationship as that man's daughter was one of honor. As young as I was, I honored him because he was such a trustworthy man. Above all, I didn't want to disappoint him."

If you ever wondered how much impact a father can have on a daughter, I urge you to travel to Bellingham, Washington, and look into the eyes of Shirli Hunt. The decades haven't even begun to dim her passionate respect, love, and honor for the man who raised her.

In all my years of practice and of speaking to literally millions of people through radio and television and at seminars, one fact has impressed me as much as anything else: Fathers leave an indelible imprint on the lives of their daughters. They shape their daughters in ways so profound that many women live with unwritten rules they've never thought to question. These rules were ingrained into them so deeply, many women don't realize that though they may graduate from college, get married, and even give birth to a half-dozen males, they'll still never stop being Daddy's girl.

A woman's relationship with her father, more than any other relationship, is going to affect her relationships with all other males in her life—her bosses, coworkers, subordinates, sons, husband, brothers, pastors, college professors, and even Hollywood movie stars. (You tell me if a woman chooses Dennis Rodman over Michael Jordan, and I'll give you an accurate picture of her father!) There's not a single relationship that isn't indelibly stamped—for good or for ill—by the man known as Daddy.

Though this book is written primarily for men, I know a number of women will pick it up just to see what we men are talking about. If you are one of these women, I think you'll discover the depth of one man's imprint on your life. By understanding the father-daughter bond, you'll be able to help repair a damaged heart or strengthen the blessings of a healthy relationship. You'll gain new insight into your marriage and become a better mother to your sons.

For the men, well, guys, allow me to let you in on a little secret: You have no idea how much you can improve your love life simply by being a good parent to your wife's daughters. Whenever I tell inspiring father-daughter stories during my seminars, I am treated to a loud and spontaneous feminine "ahhh."

Women just can't get enough of these father-daughter stories, and most men don't realize what they're missing by not paying more attention to their little girls. If you want a sexually eager wife, take your daughter on a date. You may be follicly challenged, with just a few strands of hair desperately clinging to a shining crown. You may carry enough extra pounds to keep a hot-air balloon on the ground (all by yourself)! But if you show appropriate love and affection to your daughter, I guarantee you that your wife will find herself sighing, "I'm so glad I married that man." (And she may even think up some very creative ways to tell you that.)

The father-daughter relationship is the key to every woman's aching heart. It's the genesis of every grown woman's sighs. It's also, unfortunately, the missing ingredient in many lost souls.

An Essential Ingredient

My daughter was determined to bake her parents a cake on their anniversary, and she didn't want any help. She could do it herself, thank you very much.

It was awful, to tell you the truth, just plain awful. But I knew the day would come when this daughter of mine would be able to make chocolate chip cookies and cakes that actually tasted good, so I didn't want to discourage her on her first try.

Of course, matters weren't helped by the fact that she *broiled* the cake instead of baked it.

"I just turned the oven *on*," she explained. "How was I supposed to know the other dial was set to broil?"

Fair enough. After she scraped off the top crust, the "cake" was about an inch high. She piled it with frosting to remind us that it wasn't brownies, then served a piece to my wife and me.

"This is so . . . *moist*," Sande, my wife, said. "I can't believe how moist this is."

"Delicious, honey," I added. "Just delicious. Could I get another cup of milk? . . . While you are at it, why don't you just bring the entire carton?" Our daughter's smile was worth the deception.

The next morning Sande was rummaging through the cupboards. "Where's the powdered milk?" Sande asked. "I bought a whole box just a few days ago, and now I can't find it."

"Powdered milk?" my daughter asked.

Sande turned around just in time to see my daughter's eyes dart quickly to the infamous "cake."

"You mean that wasn't flour?" my daughter asked.

Sande burst out laughing, and our daughter joined her. No wonder the cake seemed so moist!

Cakes are relatively easy to make, but if you change just one essential ingredient, like flour, the result will be a disaster. The fundamental ingredient in any woman's life is her relationship with her father. If that is missing or distorted, she will have to spend a good bit of time and energy overcoming the deficit.

Research clearly demonstrates that a father sets up a daughter for success. Normally, I'm not a big fan of "professional research," as I've discovered that most professional opinions resemble armpits: Everyone has at least two of them, and they usually stink. Most psychologists and social scientists couldn't agree on how to spell *father*, much less describe one accurately, but there is one thing that brings them to consensus. Rutgers sociologist David Popenoe, author of *Life*

Without Father, wrote, "I know of few other bodies of evidence (in social science) that lean so much in one direction as does the evidence about family structure."[1]

That evidence shows that a father's relationship to his daughter is one of the key determinants in a woman's ability to enjoy a successful life and marriage. Popenoe says that involved fathers boost academic achievement, promote psychological health, increase a child's empathy for others, and even bolster the status of women! If more men were involved in their daughters' lives, he asserts, more women would be leading national governments, and fewer women would be frequenting shelters for abused spouses.

Ernestine Brown, who studies African-American families at the University of California at Berkeley, warned, "Without warmth and support from their fathers, girls may grow up feeling isolated or aggressive."[2]

Always eager to catch the next wave, politicians have gone after the role of fathers in a big way. Republican Vice President Dan Quayle set off a firestorm in the early 1990s when he attacked a sitcom, *Murphy Brown*, which insinuated that fathers don't matter and that intentional single motherhood is okay. Within months, newly-elected Democratic President Bill Clinton joined the chorus supporting Quayle's contention, saying, "The biggest social problem in our society may be the growing absence of fathers from their homes, because it contributes to so many other social problems."

Conservatives may have a hard time accepting much of what political strategist James Carville says, but at least he understands the father relationship: "Number one is, the paycheck, stupid. Number two is, daddies matter, big time."

And a 1999 Teen/Parent Drug Survey found that teenagers who live in two-parent families and have fair or poor relationships with their dads are at a 60 percent greater risk of smoking, drinking, and using drugs than teens from single-mother households.

In this fifth annual survey, financed by the National Center on Addiction and Substance Abuse (CASA) at Columbia University, 71 percent of teens said they had excellent or very good relationships with their mothers, but only 58 percent reported such relationships with their fathers.

Joseph Califano Jr., former U.S. secretary of Health, Education, and Welfare and current president of CASA, said these statistics should be a "wake-up call for dads across America" to become more engaged with their children.

Unfortunately, many dads still leave child-rearing up to their wives and assume that the voice of the father can't add anything more.

"We can't leave it up to Mom," Califano cautioned. "She's doing a terrific job, but she can't do it alone."[3]

Democrat or Republican, president or pundit, people now know: Daddies *count.*

Why? Well, daddies treat kids differently; they provide a necessary complement to a mother's loving care.

Go to a public pool some time and watch a mother gently lead her child as the precious little tot floats carefree on an inner tube, calm, serene, charmed by life. The mother will invariably hold precious Buford or Betsy with two hands, carefully guiding the inner tube away from any wave higher than three inches. If she could, Mom would find a way to let her child swim without getting wet.

Now listen for the screams, and chances are, you'll find a daddy behind them. Suddenly a young girl has become a projectile, thrown out of her daddy's arms and up into the air while another eager young-ster shouts out, "Now do it to me! I'm next! Do it to me, too, Daddy!"

Mom runs up to Dad and says, "Harold, are you *sure* that's safe?"

"Ah, she's fine, Edith, she's fine. Kids this age bend; they don't break," he responds.

Mom clicks her tongue in disgust, armed with stories of at least a dozen kids who have been scarred beyond recognition by being thrown in a pool, but secretly she thinks, *I'm so glad I married that man. Look at the way he plays with his kids.*

A woman recognizes that she brings certain qualities and characteris-tics to the parenting task and that her testosterone-toting husband brings an entirely different perspective and approach, and she realizes that both an active father and mother are crucial for kids to get the best start in life.

This goes far beyond boys needing a male role model. In fact, I would argue that a child's most important relationship is the one with the par-ent of the opposite sex.

The Most Important Relationship

"Dear Dr. Leman," the letter read. "I just wanted to thank you for a great idea that you mentioned when you spoke at our church last fall. You said we should have more 'dads and daughters,' 'moms and sons' events. So I decided to give it a try, and we sponsored a Sweetheart Dinner for dads and daughters this past Friday. We had originally hoped that we would have 50 people attend. On Friday, we served dinner to 274 people! . . . Thanks again for the terrific idea!"

It's not that there's anything *wrong* with mother-daughter banquets or father-son outings; it's just that the church seems blind to the even greater importance of cross-gender relationships between parent and child. A woman's marriage says far more about her relationship to her father than it ever will about her relationship to her mother. A man's marriage is overwhelmingly influenced not by the times he played catch with his dad but by the times he spent alone with Mom.

Every husband either pays the price or reaps the rewards sown by his father-in-law. A positive example is Atlanta Falcons quarterback Chris Chandler. When Chris met Diane Brodie, the woman who became his wife—daughter of the legendary San Francisco 49ers quarterback John Brodie—he was a second or third string quarterback, just barely hanging on in the league. He had played on three teams in five years, and his future looked bleak.

Just a few years later, in 1998, Chandler threw for 3,154 yards in one season, including 25 touchdown passes, leading the Atlanta Falcons to a 14-2 regular season and Super Bowl XXXIII. The reason for Chandler's turnaround? Listen carefully to what he told *USA Today:* "I'd never had anybody like Diane to talk to, to listen to me. *She and her father are so much alike*—upbeat and high energy. They renewed my belief in myself, which allowed me to take my game to a higher level . . ."[4]

Chris benefited greatly from marrying a woman who has a great relationship with her father. That man instilled the type of personality in his daughter that helped Chris to achieve his full potential—and more.

There are also negative experiences. While Natalie Cole, daughter of the phenomenally successful singer Nat King Cole, and best-selling recording artist in her own right, loved her father dearly (she told a *Good Housekeeping* reporter in 1992 that she "adored" him), she sometimes felt "left out and jealous."

"In my child-mind there was doubt as to who my father preferred—his fans or me," she said. "It seems I was always angry or hurt because he was never around as much as I needed him to be. I wanted so much more of him than he was able to give."

Natalie had a difficult time dealing with the frequent absences of a touring father. And then, when Natalie was just fifteen years old, her father left for good, this time through death.

Nat's departure and earlier habitual absences left an indelible, negative imprint on his daughter. "Since I unconsciously thought men would leave me as my father always had, I would leave first, thereby ensuring I wouldn't get hurt," Natalie told *Good Housekeeping*. The reporter, Alan Ebert, noted, "In the decade between her first marriage and her current one . . . Natalie left every man with whom she had been involved."[5]

Both husband and wife need to know the pervasive influence passed down by the parent of the opposite sex. The father-daughter or mother-son relationship will greatly influence whom a person marries and how well they do within that marriage.

A silent, noninvolved dad leaves women clueless about men. (A distant mother leaves men without any understanding of women.) Who better to tell a young woman what is going on inside a male when she lets a boy kiss her than her very own dad, who happens to own the same equipment as the girl's suitor?

I'm constantly reminding women of something that very few of them understand on their own. A husband's primary need is sexual fulfillment. Notice I didn't say *sex*. I said *sexual fulfillment*. We'll talk about the difference in a later chapter. The way most mothers pull young brides aside and explain "the wedding night," women would never guess what I'm talking about.

Women's primary need is . . . gardening. Well, maybe not gardening, but digging around in the dirt actually did precede sex in a national study of women's preferred activities. The problem is, most women want men to intuitively understand their needs. They don't want to tell their husbands what they need; they just want their husbands to *know*. Most husbands remain clueless, and so thirty years later, when they take Junior aside on his wedding day and try to explain things, the poor young man inherits a game plan that might work on Jupiter but will have absolutely no relevance on this planet.

In both cases—with mothers talking to daughters and fathers talking to sons—ignorance is passed on like a communicable disease, and marriages become sick accordingly.

The cure? Strengthen father-daughter, mother-son relationships. Let a woman tell a young man what a young wife needs. Let a father tell a young woman what her husband wants. The successful team needs a balanced attack, both offense and defense. We need to break down the ridiculous wall that keeps both sexes divided.

This is why I often urge families to turn off the television—not because of what they'll see, but because of what they *won't* see. On today's television shows, kids won't see men of responsibility. They won't view husbands and wives who respect each other. The kids won't watch other children honor their parents. They're far more likely to see a stupid, clueless dad whom everybody puts up with and who is recognized as the family joke.

It is insidious for kids to see dads play the butt of every silly line in nightly sitcoms. Homer Simpson has replaced Ward Cleaver as America's stereotypical dad. The National Fatherhood Initiative reviewed prime-time programming on the ABC, NBC, CBS, Fox, and WB networks during the late autumn of 1998. They found that fathers are central, recurring characters on only 15 of 102 network comedies or dramas, and *only* 4 of these programs portray the dad as both competent and caring. This means that slightly less than 4 percent of prime-time television shows give an accurate portrayal of what a father should be.[6]

This has been going on for some time. Earlier in the 1990s, on the ABC miniseries *The Women of Brewster Place*, a young, shy woman laments that she doesn't have a husband. An older, "wiser" woman responds, "Well, I've had five, and you ain't missing much."

Even the evening news contains attacks on dads. One social "expert" actually suggested that, when given a choice between welfare payments and husbands, women should choose welfare payments, since welfare payments are generally more reliable and less bothersome than men.[7]

A man's importance as a father needs to be respected for the woman's well-being as much as anything else. A woman needs to reach up toward her father before she will be free to reach out toward her husband or down toward her son.

In the coming pages, we're going to further explore the tremendous difference that a daddy makes. One way for a woman to look at her father is to consider him as the man who made her what she is.

In Section Two, we'll look at "Daddy's Duty." We'll explore the marks of a healthy father-daughter relationship and we'll examine the key components involved in giving a daughter her best possible start in life.

In Section Three, "Daddy's Dilemmas," we'll touch on the difficult subjects: how a father can talk to his daughter about sex and physical development; what to do when Mom and daughter start competing for Dad's attention; and how a father can make a successful transition to becoming a father-*in-law*.

Along the way, we'll meet men and women who have struggled with these issues. And I'll tell you how I've tried to be a father to my four daughters. I have to admit, most of these stories are positive. But, hey, these are my memories. I like to see "the cub," as I call myself, as a hero. After all, there are many times when I'm not. To get the unedited version, you need to speak directly to my four girls.

Throughout the book you'll find practical help and come across a few stories that may make you laugh and even cry. But more than anything else, I hope this book will reawaken in you the wonder of the mysterious relationship that exists between a daughter and her daddy.

CHAPTER 2
That Man Matters

I still remember when Holly, my oldest child, was born. My wife and I were in the delivery room, and I was working hard to be the world's best labor coach.

I watched Sande squirm as her stomach was twisted by yet another contraction. "Everything's okay," I encouraged her, holding her hand as she lay there.

"Okay?!" She half yelled, half grunted. "Listen, buddy, things may be okay *up there*, but I assure you they're not even close to being okay *down here!*"

Sande had a gift for being acutely aware that she was the only one in the room experiencing pain.

Secretly, I suppose I thought a boy would be nice. I liked to hunt and fish in those days, and I love sports. But all of that was wiped out as soon as Holly made her entrance into the world. Holding that little girl was the most awesome experience I've ever known, and I remember thinking to myself, *She's perfect. Absolutely perfect.* I wouldn't have changed the shape of her toes, the length of her body, and certainly not her gender. She was ideal just as she was.

Sande had miscarried twice before she got pregnant with Holly, which made Holly's arrival all the more special. When we brought her home, I was well prepared. I had the house so hot you could have popped corn in the sink. No way was my little girl going to catch a cold!

"But we really don't want to cook her, do we, dear?" Sande pleasantly inquired.

It took me a while to become comfortable with this little creature. The nurse had warned me to support her head, so I always made sure I scooped her up just so, fighting back morbid thoughts that if I forgot to do so, my little girl's head would fall back into the crib like that of a poorly made doll.

I became overly fond of mirrors. Every five minutes or so, I casually held a small one under my sleeping daughter's nose, and a huge smile covered my face when I saw the life-signaling cloud of breath cover the glass.

My daughter.

What I didn't realize at the time was that this little girl would grow up all too quickly and one day look into my eyes and respond, "My daddy" with the same wistful, emotion-laden tone.

I wish there were some way I could get fathers to look away from their investment portfolios, step out of their offices, or get their heads out from under the hoods of their cars long enough to ruminate over the mystery of a father's love for his daughter and a daughter's love for her father. I believe a good percentage of a man's ultimate happiness, meaning, and fulfillment lies in that relationship.

But men, brilliant beings that we are, are like the guy at the turn of the century who never turned on his faucet but instead dug a hole in his backyard, hoping to find water. What we want is right in front of us, but we go everywhere else in search of it, missing that precious little gem who waits patiently for our attention.

Fortunately, some of our nation's most famous men are waking up to the fact that parenting can become a man's most meaningful and challenging vocation. Let's see if we can't learn a thing or two from them.

The Next Challenge for Jordan and Johnson

When Michael Jordan announced his retirement in January 1999, it made headlines around the world. A Milan, Italy, newspaper proclaimed: "Ciao, Jordan, You Will Always Be Air-Basketball!" In Tokyo, the headlines seemed apocalyptic: "Jordan Retires! Shock Felt Around the World!"

Few basketball fans will ever forget many of the incredible plays that Jordan made, but I will always remember one in particular. It occurred during Game Two of the 1991 NBA Finals against the Los Angeles Lakers. His Airness drove down the center of the lane and went up for a right-handed layup. Immediately, Sam Perkins and A. C. Green came over to cover him. They had him smothered in midair, and it looked like the greatest basketball player of all time would be seriously embarrassed, stuffed without anywhere to go.

Instead, Jordan changed his plans in midair. He seemed to defy the law of gravity, hanging in the atmosphere long enough to double-clutch and transfer the ball from his right hand to his left.

It was a split second decision that caught the two defenders completely off guard. The ball gently bounced off the backboard and fell through the net. An uproarious bellow from the crowd followed a stunned silence. It was an amazing play.

Another startling move occurred several years later during an all-star game. Grant Hill was shooting a free throw as Jordan hung back on top of the key. For 99.99 percent of basketball players, the top of the key during a free throw is usually considered a defensive position. But just as Hill let go of the ball, Jordan raced down the center of the key, beating all the players who were lined up right beside the basket, and took the ball off the rim, slamming it home without touching the ground.

Even Jordan seemed awed by this one. He smiled, wagged his head, and shrugged his shoulders as if to say, "Where did that come from? I don't know any better than you." He was six inches shorter than the centers and twenty feet farther from the ball, but the ball still ended up in his hands.

After such a spectacular and exciting career, you might think Jordan's retirement would be, well, boring. Jordan addressed this during a press conference called to announce his retirement. He referred to the fact that some questioned whether he would hate retirement because it would lack the "challenge" he needed. Jordan was adamant.

"I dispute that," he said.

What was the challenge he looked forward to, one that could measure up to the excitement of winning six NBA titles and countless individual records? Was it entering politics?

No.

What about becoming a CEO, or once again entering a new professional sport?

Absolutely not.

The challenge Michael Jordan looked forward to was . . . *parenting*.

In 1998, a researcher sought to make a name for herself by publishing a book purporting that parents really don't matter. According to her, peer influence and nature's imprint will determine a child's destiny, and there's little a parent can do about it.

As a psychologist, it was inevitable that I'd be asked about this book—which I don't want to dignify by mentioning its name. Apart from the fact that this woman didn't even have the credentials to examine the literature she collated (there were no original studies, just a collection of other studies, and she has no background in the social sciences), it's so easy to refute what this woman is suggesting.

"Let's go down to the local prison," I told one inquirer. "Let's talk to the prisoners. You show me one inmate who had a mom and dad who honored each other and had a loving, respectful marriage. I doubt you'll find one."

It almost pains me to have to remind parents of this, but the very act of parenting has come under so many assaults that it's necessary: As a father, *you make a difference.* It is not true that all parents can do is cross their fingers and hope for the best. We *can* help our children find their way in life. It is crucial that we do this.

Why don't most men see parenting for the challenge that it is? One of the most difficult aspects is that fathering never stops. Whereas Michael Jordan had a halftime to recover from weariness and a season's end to look forward to, there is no season's end or halftime in parenting. There are no time-outs, either. Michael Mignard, dean of students at Meadow Creek Christian School in Andover, Minnesota, found this out when he was driving his kindergarten-age son to a doctor's appointment.

"Dad," his son said, "Erin saw you in your car at McDonald's yesterday."

Mignard didn't know who Erin was. But Erin had passed the news on to his son, and Mignard realized he was always on display, even when he wasn't aware of it. It was a sobering realization.[1]

You might think that men would eagerly embrace such a challenge. Aren't we the ones who first tackled Mount Everest and the North Pole and sailed across wide seas to reach distant lands?

Yet all too frequently, parenting—especially *fathering*—receives the leftovers. After work, after golf, after the car gets fixed and the football game is over, then, if nothing else needs to be done, the father will make time for his children. Many men are missing out on the most fulfilling *and most influential* work they could ever do.

Miami football coach Jimmy Johnson saw the futility of the rat race in 1999, just after the Dolphins had been knocked out of the playoffs. Near the end of 1998, Johnson's mother died. There was a viewing the day before the funeral, which Jimmy wasn't able to attend due to his responsibilities as head coach, but he noted with a voice chock-full of emotion that his sons had been there.

The experience tore him up, especially after the season was over and no fewer than five out of twenty-eight—almost 20 percent—of the head coaches were fired in two days. Johnson saw that he was in a grueling profession that demanded all but gave no loyalty in return.

"I hear coaches say they put their religion first, family second, and football third," he said, "but they work at football fifteen or sixteen hours a day. They go to church one hour a week. And they spend a few hours with their families. That tells me where their attention is."

Jimmy had the excitement of coaching a very successful and historic franchise. He led a sure-to-be-Hall-of-Fame quarterback, Dan Marino. He was convinced that he was "just a couple playmakers away" from winning a championship. But more than another Super Bowl ring, he desired increased time with those he loved, so he worked out a deal with his owner to bring in an assistant head coach to lighten the load.

"I'm not going to be here at midnight anymore," the hard-charging Johnson promised.[2]

Michael Jordan and Jimmy Johnson—the ideals of successful masculinity according to our culture—both sought a change that would make family a higher priority. Yet all across this country, many men are ignoring their kids to get what Jordan and Johnson have already experienced—and found wanting.

A Man's Worth

By 1986 Sande and I had three children, the youngest of whom was nine years old. Sande was forty-two and I was forty-four. My career was taking off; finances were comfortable; life was turning out perfectly. We were ready to move on.

Life was going too perfectly, as it turned out.

Sande and I were enjoying a steakhouse dinner when she slipped me a card signaling the end of my blissful complacency. My wife is an artsy type of person, and it was just like her to produce a homemade card.

I opened the envelope and read the front of the card: "Are you ready to change your vacation? Are you ready to change your sleeping habits?"

What in the world is this? I thought. Was there a joke I was missing?

"Turn it over," Sande suggested.

I did so and read *Merry Christmas!* But it was the picture that caught my eye. There was Santa Claus holding a cute little baby with a toothless grin.

I looked at Sande and my mouth dropped open.

"Does this mean what I think it means?"

It did.

Enter daughter number three, Hannah.

Five years later, once again thinking that our family was complete, forty-seven-year-old Sande surprised me for what was surely the last time.

On this occasion, I was even less charitable. "Give me something to kill. I'll kill it right here," I muttered under my breath. I was forty-nine years old! I quickly did the math and realized that when this baby grew up and entered high school, I'd be drooling over my walker during the PTA meetings.

But today, if you ask our youngest, Lauren, to complete the sentence "You are daddy's little . . .", ten to one she'll say "gift from God."

Everything that Lauren and Hannah "disrupted" pales in comparison to what they've brought into my life, confirming to me once again that no matter what I do, I will never be more fulfilled than I am as the father of four daughters and one son.

When I walk through the front door, it doesn't matter what Lauren and Hannah are doing. They can be in the middle of eating an ice cream sundae, watching the exciting conclusion of *Little House on the Prairie*, or playing with their favorite friend; they'll drop what they're doing and make a mad dash to Dad.

These two little girls are so keyed in to the arrival of their father, they can't wait to get their arms around me. They don't care how much money I've made that day. They couldn't care less how many books I'm selling, or whether two dozen or two thousand people showed up to hear me speak. The doctorate degree behind my name means absolutely nothing to them. I could be a high school dropout (which I very nearly was), and they'd feel the same way.

One of the saddest things I've witnessed is how so many men miss this unconditional love and acceptance because they fail to nurture one of the most precious relationships they'll ever have. They spend all day fighting for respect at the office, wearing out the leather on their two-hundred-dollar pair of shoes, just to get the world to say, "That man matters."

Let me tell you something: *If you have a daughter, you matter more than you'll ever know.* Every decision you make should take this into account. If you ever get tempted to dump your wife, do yourself a favor. Hold your daughter in your lap, look into her eyes, then just try to tell her you're going to leave. You can't divorce your wife without making your daughter feel you're divorcing her as well.

I don't care who you are. Your company can replace you (and they will), but in your little girl's eyes, there will always be just one of you.

Why expend all your energy outside the home for something that is so freely given inside? I know part of the answer. At precisely the time that most men are starting a young family, they're also climbing a couple of rungs on the corporate ladder. The time they're most needed at home is the time they're pulled most strongly toward work. It's crunch time.

Pause just a moment and ask yourself: What's really most important? Of all the things you do, what will make you matter most? Do your kids really need another ten thousand dollars? Or would they benefit more from a dad who makes it home in time for dinner more often?

I do a lot of talking on radio and television shows—*The View, Oprah,*

CNN, the *Today Show*, *Good Morning America*, *Focus on the Family*. On one occasion, I brought one of my daughters with me to the studio. After the first session, I stepped outside to get a cup of coffee, but my daughter wanted to hang around.

Thinking that nothing could possibly harm her, I left my daughter alone, and when I came back, I found that the host had decided it would be "fun" to put my seven-year-old daughter on the air—without my permission.

You want to see angry? The IRS could confiscate everything I own, and it wouldn't even make it on the scale compared to how I felt about this parasite, this amoeba, this infectious disease who dared to mess with my daughter without checking with me first.

I got there just in time to hear him ask her, "What's it like to have a father like yours? One that's on television and radio all the time?"

Krissy cut me to my knees with her response. "Oh, you don't understand," she said. "He's just my daddy."

Everything that impressed that parasitic host meant nothing to my little Krissy. To her I was a waist to hug, a cheek to kiss, and two arms to enfold her. I'm a person to encourage her, a strong presence to guide her, a nurturer who will love her.

Yeah, I cried. Wouldn't you? When it comes to my daughters, I'm the biggest wuss there is.

Because my two oldest daughters are now in their twenties, I've come full circle in many ways and have gained a perspective I'd like to pass on to a few of you dads. Remember that little girl Holly I told you about at the beginning of this chapter? I'll never forget the day she went off to college. It shaped my priorities forever.

"Now It's My Turn"

The day Holly went away to college, she just about ripped my heart out. We loaded up two cars and drove two and a half hours to Grove City College, about fifty miles from Pittsburgh, Pennsylvania. Though both cars were fully packed, they were emptied within five minutes, mostly by boys who seemed to be casting enough side glances at Holly to risk neck problems for the rest of their lives.

I wondered if strangling a college boy to make a point about the sanctity of my daughter would be considered self-defense.

The day was a whirlwind of helping Holly set up her room, going to parents' meetings, and touring the campus. Finally I turned to Sande and said, "Well, we better get going."

"We can't leave yet," Sande protested. "I haven't made Holly's bed."

Remember, we were dropping Holly off at *college*, not preschool. But before I could argue, Sande shot me the look that husbands recognize to mean, "You better back off, chump."

Being a man of discretion, I backed off.

Five minutes later, the bed was made and there were no more excuses to stay. For the first time in almost two decades, one of our children would live under a different roof. Holly started to say good-bye, and I felt a lump the size of an elephant work its way up my throat.

"Don't say good-bye here," I pleaded with Holly. "Walk us out to the car."

I sort of stumbled to the parking lot, not at all liking what was going on, and watched as Sande and Holly said a few final words. Sande was hugging Holly in a cradling manner, softly rocking our eighteen-year-old, almost as if she wanted one final moment with her little baby.

I purposefully kept my distance, afraid that if Holly approached me I'd break down on the spot and make a spectacle of myself. "Don't you dare come over here," I silently muttered. "Stay right where you are."

Of course, as soon as I said that, Holly broke from her mother's arms and walked toward me. She put her arms around me and said, "I love you, Dad."

I held Holly close to me for a long time. She went to pull back, but I wouldn't let go. The symbolism was too real, and all my self-defenses were obliterated.

I started sobbing profusely.

Holly looked up at me with astonishment. "Dad?" Her mouth dropped open. "What's wrong? I've never seen you cry like that in my life!"

I looked down and saw that my tears were falling on Holly's "front." It's funny what you think about at life's most tender moments. In this case, I was reminded that Holly has breasts. In a split second, my thoughts went back to when Holly was just ten years old and I found myself stepping on something that was lying on the floor.

I picked it up and looked at it in astonishment. At first glance it appeared to be a bra, so I assumed it belonged to my wife, yet clearly it was much too small for Sande. In amazement and great curiosity I carried that thing around the corner and called out to Sande, "Honey, what's this?"

"That's Holly's bra."

I looked at that thing again and shook my head. "My Holly has a bra?" Then I kind of chuckled. "This looks like it's going to grow up someday and *become* a bra."

Holding my daughter in the parking lot, I kept thinking, *You can't be grown up. You're still ten years old. No, you're twenty and a half inches long, and I'm just bringing you home from the hospital, turning up the heat, and checking your breathing every ten minutes.*

This can't be. We need more time together. I'm not ready to wake up on Saturday mornings and not see you in front of your cereal bowl. Will anybody else eat Cocoa Puffs?

Then my testosterone kicked in. When men get choked up and emotional, we tend to shut down.

"Holly, you gotta go," I said, turning her around and giving her a gentle nudge. She walked away from me in a straight line, never looking back.

"Holly, call us tonight, honey!" I called out.

Holly lifted her hand above her shoulder, like a politician waving off a reporter's question, and disappeared into the dormitory without turning around.

I looked at Sande and said, "Let's get out of here." We drove in silence for twenty minutes, holding hands, thinking, grieving. Everything within me screamed, "Flip a U-turn, Leman, and get that girl of yours out of there. Forget this college stuff. She belongs at home."

Somehow our car kept heading north and we made it back to Chautauqua Lake.

That night I lived for Holly's phone call. When a ring broke the silence, I about tackled everyone trying to get to the phone. The call was for Krissy.

"Five minutes," I told her. "Holly's gonna call, and we don't want to hold up the line."

Krissy knows when I'm not being fully rational, so she kept to her limit. I immediately checked for messages in case Holly had called while Krissy was on the line, but there were none.

I went back to the living room and waited.

"Holly knows I watch the evening news," I said. "Maybe she's waiting until it's over."

Eleven-thirty came and I waited some more.

And I went to bed.

Holly never called.

The next day, Monday, I was home early. Clearly, Holly had gotten hung up the night before, I thought, but she'd call us tonight. As a former dean of students, I knew enough not to call her, but oh, how I couldn't wait for her to call me.

Up till that moment, I had never in my life looked forward to a phone ringing, but that night and the next six days there wasn't a sweeter—and then sadder—sound.

The phone rang all right, but Holly wasn't behind a single call.

The next Sunday—seven days after we had dropped her off—Holly finally called. I was excited, but I told myself to cool it lest I scare her off. Instead, I let her ramble on about freshman week, the campus, and how beautiful Pittsburgh is. Toward the end of the conversation, she turned a little melancholy. Finally I couldn't help myself.

"Holly," I said. "I've got to ask you a question. When you were walking away from us last Sunday, what were you thinking about?"

"Daddy," she said—and I immediately noticed she didn't say Dad—"It's funny you should mention that, because I was thinking about it all this week. What was going through my mind was, *Well, Mom and Dad really brought me up right, and now it's my turn to go do it.*"

Now it's my turn. That's what fatherhood is all about—giving our kids their turn. The greatest accomplishment I could ever undertake is preparing the next generation to take over their world. Any sacrifice I had made on Holly's behalf, at that moment, seemed so insignificant to the woman she had become.

I got a letter from Holly a few days later. Since I know I could never survive reading it at a seminar, I thought I'd put it in this book.

Dad,

I hated saying goodbye to you. I didn't think it'd be that hard for either of us—especially you. I really miss you, Dad. It's weird, these past two weeks I've felt closer to you than ever just because I saw how much you were going to miss me.

I miss waking up and reading the newspaper with you the most. I *loved* having you all to myself, early in the morning, sitting on the counter and reading and discussing the paper with you. I *really* liked the way you handed me the "Life" and "Dear Abby" sections before I asked for them. I'll bet you miss me walking in on you when you're taking a shower!

Thanks for all your encouragement, Dad. Whenever I feel discouraged, I think of all the times you wanted to quit but didn't. I'm very proud of you and all you've accomplished.

Dad, I love you so much. You're the best dad in the world! Thank you for giving me an education.

Never forget how much you mean to me.

I love you!
Holly

Years later, I told the story of my and Holly's parting at a seminar Holly happened to be attending. Afterward, Holly came up to me and said, "You know, there's something missing in your story."

"What's that?"

"You know why I didn't turn around?" she asked.

"No. Why?"

"Because I was crying, and I didn't want you to know I was scared."

Holly knew she was loved. She knew she had been given a good start. And now she wanted me to be proud of her. She didn't want me to know she was afraid because she knew it was time for her to step out on her own.

Holly may have been scared, but she did fine. She went on to become an attendant in the homecoming court her freshman year and in her senior year as homecoming queen. If I've given you the impression I came anywhere near to being a perfect father, let me tell you the mistake I made when Holly was crowned queen at Grove City College.

I had accepted a Parent Talk Seminar with Randy Carlson, long before we knew that Holly would be a queen candidate.

Once Holly had been chosen as a finalist, I told Randy, "Hey, I need to leave the seminar early so I can attend the homecoming ceremonies at Grove City College. Holly is running for queen, and at a small college like this, there's a big to-do. A parade. The homecoming game. The dance. I can't miss it."

Randy understood how I felt, but several hundred people had already signed up for our seminar, which was to include both of us for the entire time. "How can I tell them you'll only be here for a day?" he asked.

Rather than stick to my guns, I stood behind my former commitment.

Then Holly was elected homecoming queen, and I was not there to share that special event with her.

I wish I had said, "I am leaving anyway," but I didn't.

I know Holly wishes I had done so.

I'm certainly proud of that honor and everything else she's done. She went through commencement with no fewer than six job offers on the table. Today, she chairs the English department at a local high school. She's making the most of her turn.

It's my daughters' and my son's turn now, and I feel prouder about giving them a good start than anything else I've ever done. I don't have to prove that I count; I just need to look in the right direction and I'm immediately reminded that I do.

Parting Shots

I don't know how to say this without just coming out with it, so here it is: My wife is a looker. Men, if she walked into the room, you'd notice her.

Twice.

Which means that whenever she's standing next to me, men invariably let their eyes roam from me to her, and back to me, and I can read the wheels turning in their minds: *How did a guy like him get a woman like her?*

I'm not sure that men ever outgrow the need to be wanted by women. But often we focus on being wanted for the wrong things.

We think if we make enough money, we'll be wanted. And you know what? We will be. By materialistic women. Or we imagine that if we can have the abdomen and chest of a twenty-five-year-old when we're fifty-five, women will take notice. But they'll be shallow women who care about such things.

It is far more meaningful to be appreciated for our character. I can't tell you how many women come up to me after my seminars, tears streaming mascara down their faces, whispering, "I wish you could be my dad." It's very often a grown woman who says this. She'd never imagine me as a husband—I'm not a looker—but boy, would she like to go back and have me for a dad.

Bob Carlisle, who wrote and recorded the popular song "Butterfly Kisses," has had the same experience. In his book by the same title, Bob wrote, "I get a lot of mail from young girls who try to get me to marry their moms. That used to be a real chuckle because it's so cute, but then I realized they don't want a romance for Mom. They want the dad who is in that song, and that just kills me."[3]

That's how deep the father hunger is in a woman's heart. This isn't just sentimental wishing. Dr. Kimberlyn Rachael Anne Leary did a doctoral dissertation on a father's impact on his daughter during adolescence. Even when the father was perceived to be distant and less involved, the adolescent daughter viewed her father as "larger than life" and as "having considerable psychological presence" in her life.[4]

At my funeral I want just two things. First, a lot of crying would be nice; wailing would be preferable. Let the whole town hear that at least a few people are sad to see Cubby Leman go into an eternal hibernation as far as this world is concerned.

But second, I'd like my wife to say I was a good husband and a good father.

Don't bury me with my books. For crying out loud, don't even *think* about putting my diplomas in my coffin. Let me be buried with the memories of those I love the most. Let me live on in the sparkle of my daughters' eyes and the carefully planted confidence of a grown son.

I don't need a Super Bowl ring, a fifty-year watch, or a portfolio the size of Warren Buffett's. I just want a family who misses me, grandkids who remember me, and a wife who needs and respects me.

If that comes true, I'll know I've mattered—and I'll never care what the rest of the world thinks.

CHAPTER 3

A New Meaning
to the Family Bed

Melissa, age twenty-six, was just back from her honeymoon. It was a warm summer day in Seattle, Washington, and it took all her energy to put off calling her husband until one o'clock.

"Hey, Greg, come home!" she said.

"What happened?" Greg asked. "Is something wrong?"

"No, nothing's wrong. It's such a beautiful day . . ."

"And the point is?"

"We shouldn't waste it. We should go for a walk."

"A walk?"

"Yeah."

"Hello, Earth to Melissa, I just started this job. It's one o'clock. I can't beg off just because the sun is out!"

"I don't see why not. I mean, what's the use of getting married if I'm going to see you less than when we were engaged?"

What's going on behind this conversation? Why would Melissa even think to make this call? Why couldn't Greg even begin to take her seriously?

Melissa was the youngest of five children. Her father, an auction-eer, owned his own business. Except for the ironclad responsibility of being at the Wednesday night auctions, he had absolute control over his own time. If the weather was unusually nice—which, in the Seattle area, was not exactly a daily occurrence—he would often take the afternoon off and spend time with his wife and two youngest daughters.

Melissa brought an unwritten "rule book" into her marriage, and one of those rules was that husbands can take off work any time they want.

You'd think couples would exchange their rule books before they walk down the aisle, but they rarely do. Most couples aren't even aware that the rule books exist—until they start their new home and decid-ing whether to place the garbage pail under the sink or out on the porch suddenly turns into World War III.

Once you walk down that flower-strewn aisle, almost as soon as you finish combing the last piece of rice out of your hair, reality sets in. And guess what? Life happens. *Your husband violates a rule!*

Melissa was living in her own customized fantasy. She assumed that a twenty-eight-year-old husband/employee would have the same freedom as a fifty-five-year-old small business owner. She had to learn that marriage is not like dating. After marriage, a cement truck full of responsibilities gets dumped on the couple's front porch: pay-ing off a mortgage, buying your own groceries, setting up a household of your own. To successfully navigate the stormy waters of this tran-sition, couples must create new rule books adapted to their particu-lar situation.

This gets even more difficult when you realize that more than just two people are inhabiting the marriage bed.

A Crowded Bed

When two people marry, at least six individuals are coming together—the bride and groom, plus two parents on each side. If blended families are involved, the numbers can grow to ten or more, depending on how many remarriages there were. These groupings do not physically reside under the same roof, but their presuppositions, assumptions about life, values, and priorities will all be fighting for attention—even if one or several of the individuals are dead.

Couples ignore childhood influences at their peril. Every person brings a rule book to life and marriage, and the more rule books there are, the more likely an unsuspecting spouse is going to break a rule. A simple tool called *lifestyle analysis* helps couples become aware of and evaluate the rule books previously taken for granted. Lifestyle analyses are helpful in large part because a dad's influence on his daughter is the strongest determinant of what her rule book says. If a daughter doesn't learn to evaluate the rule book she inherited from her father—or if a husband doesn't learn to understand the rule book his father-in-law passed down to his wife—the marriage bed will seem crowded indeed.

The need for a lifestyle analysis became apparent early in my own marriage.

"That's not a crescent wrench, Kevin," my wife scolded me. "That's a monkey wrench. I need a five-sixteenths."

Sande's father was very handy. I had to spend the first five years of my marriage feverishly memorizing the names of tools so I'd know which one to bring Sande. When it comes to fixing things, my hands resemble ten big toes.

At first this was a problem. Sande soon realized that if something can't be fixed with duct tape, I'm useless.

In most marriages, a wife would consider this a "strike." *You're breaking the rule book, buddy. Husbands know how to fix things. Two more strikes and you're out.* A wife naturally expects her husband to function like the key man in her life—good old Dad—and it's quite a shock when that doesn't happen.

My desire to help couples get through these misunderstandings led me to develop the process of leading them through a lifestyle analysis. First, we go through the wife's birth order. That immediately sets the stage and provides clues for why the daughter had the relationship that she did with her father. Next, we get a description of her mom and dad, searching for the underlying assumptions that have ingrained themselves in the daughter's thinking. We then follow up with a briefer description of each sibling.

As part of this process, I ask the woman to recollect some childhood memories. One of Melissa's favorites was the time her father took her shopping for her sixth birthday. It's the only time she can remember being somewhere alone with her dad. Even though her mom ultimately had to take back everything they bought (nothing fit), Melissa's eyes sparkle as she recounts the trip. Melissa can even tell you what she had for lunch (hot dog and milk, with sundae for dessert) and provide virtually a minute-by-minute recounting of a trip that took place twenty years ago.

The interesting thing is, this is the memory Melissa holds on to, *even though it was a rare* (in fact, unique) *event.* It has shaped the way she thinks men can and should function.

A lifestyle analysis doesn't need to take a long time. During a session in my office, we can usually go through it in twenty minutes. In the midst of a seminar, I'll do it in eight minutes. When I'm speaking to a large group, I like to have fun. As a woman describes her child-hood memories, I'll write down attributes of her husband—without letting her see them. After she's finished, I'll turn the board around so the audience can see what I've written but the woman still can't. I'll then ask the woman to describe her husband. The audience is amazed—in almost every case, it will appear as if the woman is read-ing off the board I've just written on.

How do I do this? A daughter tends to remember things that are con-sistent with how she views life. An older child, for example, will tend to pull up negative memories ("I got in trouble," "I skinned my knee," "I fell off my bike"). A younger sibling often has happier, more fun-lov-ing recollections ("I remember Christmas when I was four years old and I came downstairs and there was the Barbie doll I'd always wanted"). Now, we're talking about relatively healthy families here. Dysfunction can radically affect a person's recollections.

Melissa remembers her shopping trip because it's consistent with how she views life. Even though going out with her dad (alone, any-way) wasn't a common occurrence, she believes that a man can (and should) spend time with her at her convenience. She'll look for a man to marry whom she perceives to have the same qualities, but the ten-sion arises because a young woman's and a young man's perceptions are notoriously inaccurate. Each usually marries someone neither of them knows nearly as well as they think they do.

Not everybody has an opportunity to sit down with a psychologist and go through a lifestyle analysis, however, so let's talk briefly about how you can draw your own life map and begin to rewrite your own father-daughter rule book.

This is one chapter, men, that I encourage you to have your wife read. It will help both of you to better understand not only how you can raise healthy daughters, but also how your own marriage has been shaped and formed by your wife's experience with her dad.

Drawing Your Own Life Map

I have a little assignment for you. Take a piece of paper and write *Mom* on the top. In just a few words, describe your mom's personality. Don't worry—you won't show this to her, so be absolutely honest. This is not the time to describe the parent you wish you had (we'll get to that later), but to describe the parent you actually had.

This exercise will help provide you with a somewhat objective view of your mother-son experience. You can use it to ask yourself, "Am I paying the price or reaping the benefit of a good relationship with my mom (which is similar to the ties that bind a father-daughter relationship)?"

You might also use this exercise to evaluate your relationship with your dad—and then your own parenting. How would you characterize the relationship between you and your daughter? What do you suppose she is learning about life and men from the way you are treating her? Have you been affirming or critical of her?

I think I might have done fairly well with at least one of my girls. Just before she got married, Krissy wrote me a note that said, "You have made me who I am." If your daughter wrote that to you, would it be an accusation or an affirmation? Would the words be written with affection or bitterness? Doing this exercise is like doing a medical check-up—you're just making sure that everything is working properly between you and your daughter.

Please understand, men—your wife is someone's *daughter*. (You might ask her to do the same exercise, analyzing the relationship between her and her dad.) As such, she has *learned* to become the way she is. It's helpful to understand this as you try to relate to your spouse and children. If your wife's father was critical, a lifestyle analysis might help her say, "I think I told lies to myself about how I grew up. I now see that I was never good enough for my father. I do so well in life, but there's something inside of me that clobbers me on the head even when I excel. Now I can say, 'Oh yeah, with my dad it was never good enough. I couldn't even wash the car right.' He had time for my brother, but never for me."

Armed with this understanding, your wife can begin to discard her feelings of inferiority. She'll need to rewrite her rule book so that she can relate to you, her husband, in a different manner.

Maybe you married "Daddy's little princess." Perhaps your wife's father spoiled her, and you now realize that she has somewhat of a weak personality. Maybe she has been ingrained to think, *I can manipulate a man and get anything I want.* If you're a man who is married to a woman with this mind-set, you'll often feel run over. She may use tears, feigned illnesses, or even tantrums to get her way, but you'll notice that she *always* gets her way. Both husband and wife will have a lot of work to do to be able to come to terms with the unhealthiness of this style of relating. "Little princess" will need to learn how to become a compromising colleague with her husband rather than a tempestuous tyrant.

Once you've nailed down your mom's and dad's influence, it's helpful to round it out with your siblings' imprint. They have affected you—and your wife—much more than you realize.

The Role of Siblings

Do you think Bill Gates is a firstborn or later-born? Astute observers can surmise the correct answer: He's the second of three children.

"I knew Bill Gates wasn't a firstborn as soon as I heard that he dropped out of Harvard after his sophomore year over the objections of his parents," Frank Sulloway, a research scholar in the science, technology, and society program at the Massachusetts Institute of Technology, told *Forbes* magazine. "A firstborn would never do that. He would have stuck it out to get a degree and please his parents."[1]

It's not hard to see how a man who would challenge his father would also be willing to take on industry-leading IBM—and win. Firstborns may take risks, but they tend to take very calculated risks. Middle-borns are much more likely to put everything they have into a venture, even if it means distancing themselves from their dad.

Where you are in your family has affected the relationship you have with the most influential person in your life. To fill out your life map and birthprint, it is essential that you consider the influence of your siblings, so let's do for our siblings what we just did for our parents. Get out another piece of paper and describe each sibling, beginning with the older one. Include yourself in this exercise.

After you've completed your list, go back and "listen" to the role of the oldest child (even if that was you). Look for a one- or two-word summation that describes how she (or he) positioned herself with your father.

Well, she was really smart and responsible, you might be thinking.

If I were with you, I might suggest, "She was always in control, right? Always felt responsible. A good caregiver, always a giver, never a taker; whatever Daddy wanted, she was the first to buckle under and give it to him."

"How did you know that?"

"Happens all the time." Though I won't always say this, I can tell you exactly who this type of daughter is likely to marry—if she's not careful, he'll be a loser, someone who needs to be taken care of.

"Now tell me about the next one," I'll go on.

"He was the rebel. Rode motorcycles. Experimented with drugs."

"That's easy then. We'll call him the rebel. What about the third?"

"My sister? She was hyper-religious."

"The saint."

"That's it!"

"Good, we'll mark her down as the saint. And you?"

"Loved sports. Very athletic."

Wherever you are in this family, you can begin to understand why you are the way you are. The saint can understand that the rebel role was already taken. If she wanted to be noticed by others, *especially by Daddy*, she had to do something different. Whereas the rebel (who couldn't compete with the firstborn) took delight in disappointing Daddy (because that's how he got noticed), the saint got her kicks from never eliciting Daddy's disapproval.

In my own family, my sister received straight A's. My brother was the quarterback. What was left for me? Academics and athletics were spoken for. I became the family clown. I wasn't certain I could make my father proud, but I was sure I could make him laugh.

Siblings transform us more than we would like to admit. They affect the silliest things, down to the types of movies we enjoy watching.

In my seminars, I like to ask the question, "How many women here have watched the movie that should have received four stars but only received one and a half—*The Three Amigos*—and can honestly say they loved it?"

Out of about twelve hundred people, six women will raise their hand.

"Stay with me," I'll say, and I walk out to the audience. I go up to the first woman. "Tell me, what is your birth order?"

"Youngest."

"And you have older brothers, right?"

"How'd you know?"

"We'll get to that in a moment."

Then I'll go to the next woman. "What is your birth order?"

"Middle born."

"Older brothers?"

"Yes, that's right."

I'll find another. She might surprise me.

"I was a firstborn, with no brother and just one sister."

"Really? Can you tell me in just a few words, what was your relationship with your dad like?"

"I can do that in one word. *Awesome.*"

I'll then talk to the crowd. "I know this sounds a little strange. Some of you are disappointed that a credentialed psychologist would even *go* to *The Three Amigos*, much less like it, but let me explain: *The Three Amigos* is a guy's movie from start to finish. The first time I saw it, I just about died with laughter. Then I glanced at my wife and saw her arms crossed, looking at me with a glare that screamed, 'I can't believe you're laughing at this.' I can gauge a woman's comfortableness with men in general just by how she reacts to that movie."

I knew these women generally had big brothers because a woman with older brothers will naturally be attracted to things that men are interested in. This not only makes it much more plausible that she can have intimacy with a man; it also means she'll simply enjoy being around men. Sometimes she'll even choose a man's company over a woman's.

If you're married to a woman like this, you might find it shocking that while all the other wives in a social gathering are hovering in groups of women, your wife is surrounded by men—and they're all laughing and enjoying themselves thoroughly. This doesn't mean your wife is a flirt; it means she probably grew up around men and simply prefers their company.

Guess what? Your father and your wife's father are men. No surprise there, but the more comfortable a woman is around men, the more comfortable she'll be with her father (and later with her husband). She's far more likely to enjoy fishing or hunting with her dad, which will make it easier for her dad to show affirmation to her and give her a more positive father-daughter experience.

On several occasions I have been invited to appear on the *Today* show. One time, without knowing Katie Couric's background, I said to her in the studio, "Let me guess, Katie, you must have at least three older siblings, and I'm gonna guess that some must be brothers."

I was right. She was shocked. But if you watch as she relates to men, it is patently obvious. Katie is so comfortable with the men she interviews. She easily banters back and forth and sometimes reaches over and puts her hand on their arm to encourage them.

The purpose of this lifestyle analysis isn't for you to excuse yourself or to win an argument, but for you to understand what you really feel about things and why. You can't build a successful marriage if you aren't sure about what is most important to you.

This analysis also helps you understand why you relate to the opposite sex the way you do and can provide insight as to why your spouse reacts in certain ways. When you know what you expect from your spouse, you are then able to express these expectations, revise them, or discard them. At the very least, your expectations won't rule over you.

Most couples need to get better at zeroing in on how they feel about what's going on in their marriage. Otherwise, they live with an unrecognized aura of frustration *and never really know why*. They keep burying the dissatisfaction until one day it erupts into an affair, a bitter argument, or another harmful behavior.

You might hate your mother or your father. You might love them dearly. You might feel inferior just thinking about them. You may experience any number of emotions, but whether you like it or not, *the truth is that your mother and father have had a major impact on you.* Whether you responded out of love or rebellion, you were shaped by this response. Unless you get to know *why* you responded the way you did and how your parents, particularly your mom, affected you, they will continue to rule over you—for good or for ill.

CHAPTER 4

Daddy Attention
Deficit Disorder (DADD)

Five-year-old Pamela Hollingworth wandered away from a family picnic wearing nothing but overalls and sneakers. Without a coat, she was ill prepared for the New England wilderness. For eight excruciating days, four hundred rescue workers covered the White Mountain National Forest searching for her. During this time, Pamela existed solely on handfuls of water retrieved from mountain brooks. When she was finally found and placed in her father's arms, her first words were, "Daddy, I've been waiting for you."[1]

Your daughter may never be lost in the woods, but she's waiting for you to seek her out every day in so many other ways. A little girl is constantly asking her dad, in her actions if not her words, How important am I to you, really?

One day a number of years ago, Krissy and I were enjoying breakfast at the Village Inn restaurant in Tucson, Arizona. A man came up to me and said, "Wow, you're Dr. Leman, aren't you?"

"Yeah."

He seemed so eager, I was afraid I owed him money or something.

"This is just great," he said. "I've been asked to find a speaker for our men's retreat on May 16."

Immediately I received a sharp kick to the shins, delivered discreetly, but quite forcefully, under the table. (May 16 just happens to be Krissy's birthday.)

I thought I owed it to the man to be polite and not interrupt him. He went on and on about how his church wanted the best possible speaker and that he was convinced it had to be me. He also mentioned the considerable sum they were willing to pay. Before he paused, I received another sharp kick. I didn't know Krissy's legs were that strong.

"It's very kind of you to think of me," I finally told the man, "but I have an important engagement on May 16. That day just happens to be my daughter's birthday."

I heard an audible sigh across the table. By her kicks, Krissy was telling me, "Daddy, I was waiting for you."

Unfortunately, in many families Dad never shows up. He might not do something as radical and overtly damaging as divorcing his wife and moving away from his kids, but he's just never emotionally present for his daughters.

This creates a syndrome I call *Daddy Attention Deficit Disorder*, or DADD for short. To your little girl, the world is a wilderness. She feels lost, and she's waiting for you to show up and help her get through it.

But here's the catch: Dads must learn to guide their daughters out of this wilderness rather than to carry them through it. You may think that too little attention is bad and be tempted to go to the other extreme—to do everything for your daughter, parenting her too much.

Unfortunately, as we're about to find out, that's just as dangerous.

Too Much or Too Little?

Though fathering can be measured on a spectrum, for the sake of simplicity let's look at the two poles: fathers who "overparent" and fathers who "underparent."

Fathers Who Overparent

"Dad!" Then sixteen-year-old Krissy tried to speak over the noise in the background. "What time do you want me home? The game just got over, and we're going out for pizza."

"I trust you, honey," I said. "Just be home at a reasonable time."

"What time is that?"

"You know what a reasonable time is."

I hung up before she could continue the conversation.

Ten minutes later, Krissy called again. "Dad, we're at the pizza place now. It's pretty crowded, but the basketball team hasn't arrived yet. What time should I come home?"

"Do I have two daughters named Krissy," I asked, "or didn't we just have this conversation?"

"Come on, Dad."

"I told you, Krissy. Come home at a reasonable time. You know what a reasonable time is."

"But Da—"

Click.

Within seconds, the phone rang *again.*

"Dad, don't hang up—"

"Who *is* this?"

"It's Krissy, Dad."

"Oh, the sixteen-year-old mature daughter who knows the difference between a reasonable time to get home—given the circumstances—and an unreasonable time?"

There was a long sigh. Krissy was home one hour later.

Sometimes, kids don't want to grow up. It can be a painful process for a daughter to begin making her own decisions, and some dads are all too eager to delay that process until the daughter is on social security: "You're sixty years old, Martha; it's time to start handling your own affairs."

A dad who overparents will smother his daughter. He is positive he knows just how his little girl should turn out, and he'll raise her to be like a seal that claps its hands when Daddy holds out a fishy little morsel. This will leave her always seeking Daddy's ever-elusive approval and having little or no confidence in herself.

When a father overparents, he doesn't give his child an opportunity to develop her inner resources. She becomes unduly dependent on her dad and will never be able to fully leave. Rather than enter her marriage as a full-fledged partner, she will make her husband feel like he has another child on his hands.

The marks of overparenting are these. Instead of helping a daughter form her own opinions, an overparenting dad berates any idea that differs from his own. Instead of encouraging his daughter to become responsible, the overparenting dad encourages her to stay dependent. Instead of teaching his daughter to develop her strengths and abilities, an overparenting dad criticizes and coddles his daughter to such an extent she doesn't believe she *has* any strengths or abilities.

Rather than letting a daughter contribute to the family, an overparenting dad makes her feel like a leech, living off others. This can be tragic. When a child doesn't have the opportunity to give back to the family, she is hindered from developing a crucial sense of belonging. If your child feels she really belongs, you have gone a long way toward ensuring she will not experiment with drugs, develop an eating disorder, get pregnant out of wedlock, or wind up in jail. If she doesn't feel that she belongs, she will lack the stability to avoid falling in with the wrong crowd.

The long-term effects of overparenting are equally dire. One study found that controlling, rejecting fathers may contribute to hysteria in adult women, leading to irrational angry outbursts, dependency and helplessness, and a tendency to use manipulative suicidal threats. According to the researcher, women with this trait "frequently occupied a special place in their families" and "learned to get their own way by manipulating their parents." In adulthood these women continue to be "anxious, unhappy little girls who seek a strong, idealized father-husband to take care of them."[2]

Fathering is a stage as much as it is a relationship. My role as father will take a dramatic turn when my daughters are married. In truth, however, our roles and relationships have been gradually changing almost since the day each girl was born. Day by day, week by week, and year by year, I began to dole out a little more independence and responsibility, and I drew back when I suspected that a daughter was becoming overly dependent.

I remember one moment very clearly. Holly had started dating a guy who had my radar up from the first time I met him. He seemed just a little too smooth and packaged for my tastes, and I sensed that there were serious issues in his life that needed to be confronted.

I let Holly know about my initial reaction but nevertheless welcomed her new friend into our home. A number of months later, Holly was reevaluating her relationship. She had begun to recognize the problems that I first suspected, but now that the two of them had a history together, she wasn't certain she wanted to blow that off.

Finally, we took a long drive, and Holly half cried and half said, "If you tell me not to marry this person, I won't do it, because I'm too confused and I trust you."

Every fiber in my being was quivering, but I knew I needed to handle this very carefully, so I said, "I'm going to be honest with you, Holly. I think with your strong qualities and his strong qualities, you two can pull this off, *but* you'll have a much easier time if the two of you come to the marriage table with fewer problems to overcome than he has."

I refused to absolutely tell her no, but I also registered my concerns. The decision was Holly's, and she made the wise one, ultimately ending the relationship. Because she had made the decision, however, she was willing to live with it. It made her a stronger person rather than a more dependent one.

However much some fathers might wish to overparent, eventually they will find out that overparenting just doesn't work. Children grow up. Fathers must teach their daughters how to cope as individuals if they want their daughters to succeed in life.

Fathers Who Underparent

When conflict arises in your house, instead of putting your newspaper down and getting involved in your family's life and conflict, do you simply yell out, "Martha! The kids are fighting! Would you take care of it?" Do you have any idea who your daughter's best friend is? Do you ever spend time alone with your daughter? Might your daughter feel that she has to do something extreme—like break the law or get into real trouble—in order to get your attention? You may think she's nothing but trouble, when all the while she is simply crying out, "Daddy, please notice me!"

If any or most of these are true, you may be a father who underparents. The rush of the world, the need to provide a living, the raw truth of human exhaustion, and physical limitations often collide to create extreme father neglect. This creates daughters who suffer from DADD.

Dads, imagine that someone you have never met came up to your door one evening and said, "Hey, my kid really admires that Ford Bronco sitting out in your driveway. How about letting me take it for a spin? I'll bring it back tomorrow morning as good as new."

Would any of you say, "Just a minute while I get my keys"? Of course not! And yet I meet permissive fathers who "loan out" their kids to visit overnight with a family they've never met before.

You won't loan your car, but your kid—hey, why not?

This is underparenting—treating a car as a more prized possession than a child. Our "enlightened" culture has created an industry that serves underparenting families. For instance, the same dad who wouldn't dream of loaning out his car overnight isn't bothered by the fact that someone he doesn't know any better than the mailman is spending eight to ten hours every day with his child in the *kiddy kennel*. People hate it when I call day-care centers "kennels," but that's what many of them resemble. You probably chose your children's mother— your wife—with great care; you wanted someone whom you believed was caring, reasonably intelligent, competent, and trustworthy.

But tell me—what are the names of the workers in your child's day care? How much time have you spent with them? What kind of intelligence do they model and pass on to your children? What church do they attend, if any? How concerned are they about hygiene? If you don't immediately know the answers to these questions, you are dangerously close to being an underparenting dad. In fact, the turnover rate at day cares is unbelievably high, making this type of understanding virtually impossible in the long-term.

Underparenting dads place kids low on the ladder of priorities. Even when they're home—which doesn't tend to be a big priority—these dads are often someplace else mentally and emotionally. Their children are welcome to tag along, but the dads make little or no effort to enter their kids' worlds. They don't know what music their kids listen to, what shows they watch on television, or how they spend their afternoons. All they seem concerned about is that the kids "behave" (that is, that they don't cause any trouble or commotion that would require the dad to expend a precious bit of his energy).

Children who are loved too little (victims of DADD) tend to respond to their father's distance by becoming overachievers in their vocation. The flip side of this is that their relationships are frequently a mess. They know how to succeed but not how to relate. Consequently, they become extremely competent in business or the arts and establish a solid reputation. The fuel they're running on, though, is fear that unless they keep accomplishing, they're not worth anything.

In other words, their self-esteem is shot. The connection between self-esteem and a father's love is well established. One study found that the perception of a father's unconditional regard was significantly related to a daughter's self-esteem, while only a very weak relationship was found between a woman's self-esteem and her mother's regard.[3] A Canadian study found that a father was essential for a woman to develop a sense of adequacy, self-esteem, life goals, and even feminine identification.[4]

Underparenting dads need to realize that they are emotionally and relationally crippling their children. Women who are obsessed with succeeding in order to feel good about themselves may be able to buy a big house, but the happiness they seek will inevitably elude them. They'll find themselves unable to connect intimately, as relationships are based on acceptance, loyalty, trust, and intimacy, not performance. Unfortunately, an overachiever often has a difficult time turning off the need to perform. A woman can't work herself into a frazzle all day long at the office and then suddenly stop working for approval when she gets home.

The Balanced Father

In 1976 Finland's Lasse Viren immortalized himself in Olympic history by becoming the first male to win both the 5,000-meter and the 10,000-meter races in successive Olympiads. After this stunning achievement, his coach decided to take on Emil Zatopek's record. Zatopek had won the three longest distance races—the 5,000, the 10,000, and the marathon—at the Helsinki games earlier in the century.

There was just one problem. Viren had never run a marathon before, and the Olympics aren't exactly a warm-up event. Further adding to the difficulty was Viren's understandable weariness. The guy had just won two distance races against the fastest men on earth, and now he was going to enter a marathon?

Even so, on the last day of the Montreal Olympics, there was Viren, lining up for the marathon directly behind American Frank Shorter, who had won the gold medal four years earlier in Munich.

Once the marathon got started, the waiflike Shorter found he had a shadow. Viren's coach, knowing that his country's pride had never run a marathon, much less won one, had come up with a brilliant strategy.

"Stay on Shorter's shoulder," he told his charge. "When he surges, you surge. If he holds back, you hold back."

Viren wasn't able to stay with Shorter the entire way, but the strategy proved amazingly successful. Viren placed fifth in his first marathon.

In parenting, we are Frank Shorters to our children. We've been there. We've done life before. We know what to expect. Our kids are Lasse Virens—full of talent and promise, but untried at that long a distance. The only way they know to run this race is to run it directly behind our shoulders.

That's why it is so crucial for fathers to have a balanced view of parenting. Our kids will follow us. We set the pace for their lives. If we go too fast, we'll leave them behind. If we go too slowly, they'll never strengthen their own sense of pace.

Guess what happens when a kid runs behind an overparenting father? The kid invariably rebels. Now guess what happens with the underparenting father? The kid rebels. In both cases, whether we start running the marathon too slowly or begin it running too fast, our kids will be hindered from winning if the pace we set for them is wrong.

So what does work, oh wise one from Tucson?

The healthy father must walk between these two extremes—becoming active and involved where appropriate, but teaching his daughter to build her own self-confidence and esteem in the process. He is the involved but respectful parent who allows his daughter an opportunity to give back to the family, contributing to how it is run.

Let's return to the cake analogy. The permissive father might not put in any flour. The authoritarian father might put in too much. Either way, the cake is going to be a disaster.

My mother used to make a lamb stew that was the most atrocious culinary debacle ever foisted on an unsuspecting family. The flies on the screen door used to chip in and repair the holes on the screen door when she made that stew lest any unfortunate fly meet its demise in that dastardly dish.

Some fathers are "cooking up" daughters with precisely that aroma. But fortunately, that girl will eventually grow into a woman who will have the resources—if she wants to use them—to become a gourmet person. Before she can make it right, however, she has to know what went wrong. Otherwise, the influence of the father's imprint will surface and affect her and her husband's life. This influence will be stilled only when the truth is brought out into the open.

Ideally, as a father you should encourage your daughter to go through the process of a lifestyle analysis and evaluate your style of parenting (ouch!) before she says, "I do." If not, it is likely she will marry the wrong man.

Marrying the Wrong Man

There's been a lot of speculation about Hillary Rodham Clinton, especially in the wake of so many scandalous reports about her husband. When the president subsequently confirmed that at least two of these reports were true (one occasion with Gennifer Flowers, and other trysts with Monica Lewinsky), even people who support the Clintons' policies have ruminated over how Hillary has withstood the public humiliation of her husband's infidelity. I make it a practice never to attempt to "clinically examine" people I haven't seen in counseling, but since the case is already so well known, there are some interesting factors to consider here.

Hillary's dad was a textbook, World War II-style dad. He actually trained troops for combat in the 1940s; after his stint in the military, he ran his own screen-printing plant. Hillary described him as "a self-sufficient, tough-minded, small businessman."[5]

However, he was *not* an affirming father. On one telling occasion, Hillary brought home a report card with straight A's. "My father's only comment," Hillary remembers, "was, 'Well, Hillary, that must be an easy school you go to.'"

In her book *It Takes a Village to Raise a Child*, Hillary notes, "Children without fathers, or whose parents float in and out of their lives after divorce, are precarious little boats in the most turbulent seas."[6]

What she doesn't say—but what she has unwittingly demonstrated—is that these "precarious little boats" drift into dangerous marital harbors, where they'll often receive the same treatment they've grown accustomed to as children.

As a practicing psychologist, I've found few generalizations to be all that accurate, but there's one in particular that, unfortunately, holds pretty true: Most women marry exactly the wrong man. I've seen many women scarred by their fathers who then stack the deck against themselves so these women can prove they're not worth anything—just like their father told them.

Lucy gets used and abused by her first husband, though she still manages to produce her two children in the process. Her husband treats her as badly in divorce as he did in marriage, leaving her and his children with almost nothing to live on.

Somehow, she survives. She finds a way to make life work and provide the children with some semblance of a structured home life. Of course, doing this means getting up early and staying up way past the time when her body has given in to exhaustion. Sometimes she feels like she's dependent on Tylenol and Starbucks coffee to make it through the day, but she does it.

Then she runs into man number two—typically, an older guy. Without even realizing it, she thinks this guy is like the dad she never had. She doesn't tell herself that. She doesn't understand *why* she's so drawn to his authoritarian manner. Instead, she couches his personality in overwhelmingly positive terms: He's so self-assured, so confident, so structured.

She's drawn to this man because he represents everything she lacks. Because she's never had an interested and involved father (or maybe she didn't even have a father at all), she's never developed the self-esteem that would allow her to be self-confident, assured, and secure.

She gushes to her friends about how she's finally found "the one." Sure, he might occasionally have "just a tad too much" to drink. No, he may not have the best employment record. "But he loves me; he really does."

The problem is, guy number two is "super rat," a wolf in sheep's clothing, who knows how to date *and* how to make a woman miserable in marriage. Pretty soon Lucy realizes that far from gaining the father figure she was hoping for, she's saddled with another little boy who has his own share of problems. His drinking problem turns out to be unbridled alcoholism. His spotty employment record transforms itself into the expectation that he'll live off his wife's welfare for the rest of his days.

She thought she was upgrading from a Ford to a Lexus. In reality, she bought the same old Ford with a new paint job, and before long, she'll trade him in, too. At the end of her life, she'll be amazed that every one of her six husbands was *the same man*. Some had more hair than others; some had a leaner look; but inside, every one of them was exactly the same.

To put it bluntly, Lucy migrates toward losers. This, ironically and tragically, reinforces the image she has of herself—that she's not worth loving. Otherwise, she would have found a more nurturing man, right? At least, that's what Lucy tells herself. Women who have a low view of women invariably marry men with a low view of women.

Ironically, it takes a strong father to give a woman a high view of femininity. Kids—especially daughters—get a sense from their dads that they're worth being loved. The woman who doesn't have a good self-image because she had no father or had a nonaffirming father will typically marry a non-husband or a non-affirming husband.

Men, you need to come to grips with the fact that your neglect—for whatever reason—will tempt your daughter to make a disastrous marital choice that she may pay for the rest of her life. It will also greatly affect the way she treats your grandkids.

This is another chapter I'm encouraging wives to read—for a woman's relationship with her father will indelibly stamp the way she treats her sons. Men need to be aware of this dynamic to help bring balance; women need to be aware of it to help right a family ship that is listing.

Raising the Wrong Kid

Susan is an overachieving seventeen-year-old. She is an excellent swimmer and is extremely well behaved. In today's world, being a good swimmer doesn't get you quite the respect that being able to throw a touchdown pass will, but it does provide a certain measure of self-esteem and confidence. Susan is active in student government and is a top-flight student. Few of her teachers would be surprised if she ended up running a company some day.

She came to my attention as a result of her dad and mother, who were "shamed beyond measure" by their daughter's irresponsibility and immorality. Susan was pregnant by a long-standing boyfriend.

As I talked with Susan, I discovered something that immediately caught my attention. I had picked up a hint from talking to her dad, who at first refused to talk to me. "I'm not the one who's pregnant!" he had insisted. "What do you want to talk to me for? She's the one who needs straightening out!"

I asked Susan when was the last time she had heard her dad say he loved her. Her face went ghostly white. This lovely young woman looked like a little girl with a quivering lip.

"I don't remember hearing that," she said.

"Never?" I asked.

Susan shook her head.

As we talked, I learned that Susan had drifted into the arms of an equally emotionally needy young man—interestingly, one who was almost two years older—and together they sought to find the acceptance that neither could find from the parent of opposite gender.

Except for Susan's unfortunate (and immoral) dating habits, she was everything a parent would be proud of. Yet for years she subsisted on the emotional diet of her father's critical remarks. He never mentioned her strengths, while never letting her forget her weaknesses. Susan tended to be messy. She was smaller than other kids when growing up, so they would sometimes pick on her. Rather than stick up for herself, Susan would just take it.

Susan never measured up in her father's eyes, so she got overinvolved with a young man who did something that, to Susan, seemed profound: He complimented her. He affirmed her. He made her feel like she was special, that she mattered, and that they belonged together.

The pollution of a skewed father-daughter relationship can affect several generations. The daughter grows up, becomes a mother, and (surprise!) has a skewed relationship with her own children. If the mother was criticized endlessly by her father, she may wake up one day and realize that no matter how high her son jumps, it's not high enough. He doesn't keep his room clean enough, he doesn't show enough manners, or he doesn't do well enough in school.

This is the classic case of a kid who has to be pushed at every turn. He will undoubtedly transform himself into a skilled procrastinator to protect himself from Mom's critical nature. It's really a matter of emotional self-defense. He tells himself, "I could have done a better job if I would have finished it" rather than doing his best and running the risk of Mom's flaw-picking.

The sad thing is that this boy might have ten very positive traits; other parents may openly praise him in front of the mother, but the mother will still become fixated on the two or three traits her boy is lacking. Those traits will be *all* her son hears about. He'll grow up criticized and feeling demeaned. And guess how he'll treat his own children?

Here's how to effect change. Look back at your analysis of your relationship with your daughter. Are you guilty of walking around with that high-jump bar of expectations? Do you say, "Jane, you should do this. You could do that"?

Recognize this phenomenon. Then practice saying, "I love you just the way you are" (with apologies to Billy Joel). Go out of your way to correct your imprinted tendency to criticize. Write yourself little reminders to compliment her and encourage her.

Acceptance is *crucial*. One of the most fundamental human needs is acceptance. Kids are going to belong someplace; the question isn't whether they belong, but *where* they will belong. If kids can't feel good about identifying with their home life, they will identify themselves with people outside their home. They will belong to a sports team, another family, a gang, or a girlfriend, but they'll belong somewhere.

If you were to ask each of my kids, "Who's Daddy's favorite?" I bet you they'd tell you to be quiet, pull you aside, and whisper, "Don't tell the others, but I'm sure that it's me." They all think they're the favorite—and I work to preserve that. Just a few months before Krissy got married, she gave me a copy of *Butterfly Kisses*, a book that celebrates a father's love for his daughter. After her signature, she wrote "your favorite!"

Each girl has her own place in Daddy's heart. Hannah is Daddy's little peanut. Lauren is Daddy's little muffin. One time Daddy got tired and referred to Lauren as Daddy's little peanut, and Daddy was rebuked with a vigorous, "I'm *not* Daddy's little peanut, I'm Daddy's little *muffin!*"

They guard their place in my affection with the tenacity of a people-pleasing private in the United States army. When Hannah overheard me telling someone how wonderful Lauren is, I suddenly heard this tiny throat clearing quite conspicuously: "*Ahem! Ahem!*" I looked over at Hannah and saw my fourthborn raise her eyebrows, signaling that it was about time I added, "Oh yes, I also have another wonderful daughter whose name is Hannah."

Each daughter wants to be treasured in a special place of Daddy's affection, which is why I heartily recommend giving each daughter her own nickname. One of the best gifts I can give my future grandchildren is bequeathing to them a mother (my daughter) who grows up with a strong sense of affirmation and belonging.

Will This Be Your Daughter?

Olivia, who is in her mid-forties, attended one of my seminars for singles. She stood up in front of the group when I asked for a volunteer who had suffered a really lousy marriage.

"Describe one of your parents, Olivia," I said.

"My dad is. . ."

Olivia lapsed into a painful silence. Just before it became a little too awkward, she changed tactics and said, "Well, let me you about my mom. She's controlling, a high achiever, very bossy, and pushy."

Having gotten this out, she seemed ready to tackle her father once again. "My dad, well, let's just say he really messed up. He wasn't around much."

"All right," I told her in front of the group, "let me make a guess about your ex-husband. He was a druggie, a loser, and an alcoholic."

"Go for it, doc," Olivia laughed. "You're three for three."

Suffering from Daddy Attention Deficit Disorder and being raised by a controlling mother virtually guaranteed that Olivia would bring home a "wounded dove," a weak person that she thought she had to fix, for a husband. Because her foundational "cake" was missing those all-important ingredients of a daddy's affirmation, acceptance, and presence, Olivia feels forced to prove her worth by achieving and by taking care of others. It didn't surprise me that for her vocation she chose being a nurse in an intensive care unit.

Olivia is exactly the type of person—quick thinking, competent, empathetic, trustworthy—you would want caring for you in a medical emergency. But brilliance in her profession can't overcome the ache in her soul over choosing the wrong men as husbands.

Men, I know you love your little girl deeply, or you wouldn't be taking the time to read a book like this. One day, that little girl of yours will take everything you have given her—or haven't given her—and step out into the world. Her marital satisfaction, her ability to parent her sons, her sense of well-being and acceptance will be something that she has achieved *in spite of* or in part *because of* you.

Which will it be? The cycle has to stop somewhere. If you want your father's (or father-in-law's) negative legacy to stop being passed down, why not end it with you?

Section Two
Daddy's Duty

CHAPTER 5
A Good Dad

"What seems to be the problem?" I asked, noticing that the families I counsel are getting younger and younger.

"Our baby keeps crying."

"Your baby *cries?* You're paying to visit me because you're worried about your baby *crying?*"

"Well, we're not sure if we're being too permissive, or maybe we're being too strict, and we don't want to scar this poor child *for life* by letting him cry."

"Or by *not* letting him cry," the father added hastily.

"We've done everything we could think of," the mother said. "We've been playing classical music for him for nine months now."

"I thought you said your child is four months old?" I asked.

"He is," the mom said.

"We put a speaker against Susie's stomach when she was pregnant," the husband explained. "We heard that would help the baby's brain develop."

Wow.

I've got fantastic news for you parents. You want great children?

Be a good dad. Be a good mom.

Notice I didn't say you have to be a *great* dad or a *great* mom. In most circumstances, *good* will suffice. Good will produce amazing kids. There is more margin of error for parents than most of us realize. The knots today's parents tie themselves in about their children's welfare would put an entire Boy Scout troop to shame.

I wasn't a perfect dad, but I was an involved dad, and I think I was a good dad. And good is enough.

What's happened is that we're so worried about doing the right things, we've forgotten the importance of building the right relationships. If you love your kids, they'll be confident. They'll do fine in school. They may even make it out of high school without joining a cult, jumping off a sixty-foot bridge, or ending up on the evening news.

I know, because I'm proof of it. You should see *my* ancestry.

A Well-Watered Ancestry

I come from a long line of drinkers. Virtually all the Lemans enjoyed slugging a few cold ones down. Okay, not a few. *Many.*

My father drank so much, neighbor kids used to refer to a local gin mill as my father's office. His father (my grandfather) was found dead, stiffer than a hoot owl, in a snow bank in Buffalo. He was so drunk he wasn't able to find his way home and ended up freezing to death.

Dad wasn't always the best example, but he found some creative ways to make a point. He stopped our family car one time where some men were digging a ditch beside the road.

"Hey, take a look over there," he said. "You see what those guys are doing?"

"Yeah, Dad, they're digging a ditch."

"You boys want to do that when you're older?" he asked.

"No way, Dad."

"No? Then you go to the big school (college), understand me? You go to the big school, you don't have to dig ditches."

Out of this "well-watered" ancestry came two psychologists and a children's pastor.

My mom often tells me, "I wish I'd had your books when I was raising you; I might have done a better job." But that's the point. My parents weren't particularly distinguished—my mom was a registered nurse and my dad was a hardworking dry cleaner—but our family turned out all right, and we kids still honor them.

When my father died, despite all the things we went through—particularly when I was an adolescent—and regardless of all the embarrassment Dad's drinking caused us, we missed him greatly. That was seen in the inheritance. My older brother inherited my dad's diamond ring. Of course, as the youngest born, I got Dad's nineteen-dollar ring.

But I wear it. I don't do this, of course, to make a fashion statement. I've seen plastic watches at Wal-Mart that cost more than this ring. I wear it to honor the man who wore it before me.

Early on in my life, I would never have expected myself to honor Dad. He was very imperfect, and for part of my life, especially during my teenage years, there were times when I hated his guts. By the time he died, both of us had become Christians, and we developed a very close relationship, in spite of my father's past.

If you're a good parent, you can raise great kids. You don't have to memorize fifteen secret steps. In fact, the best "secret" is to remind yourself that neither you nor your kids have to be perfect to get it right. Sometimes it's difficult for parents to see the long-term. The early years of parenting especially can seem never ending, so I like to ask these overly anxious moms and dads, "Have you ever seen someone walking around a college campus in diapers?"

"No."

"Your kid will get out of them too. It's all right that Junior's still making a mess at eighteen months. Give him time!"

You don't need a Ph.D. to figure out a child. This concern for doing the right things masks the more important aspect of building the right relationship. If you wanted to know how to build a play set, you could buy a book that would take you step by step through the process. But how does a father build a meaningful relationship with his daughter? That's a much harder question because people aren't like two-by-fours. We're not all the same. Some kids are shy. Some wear everyone around them ragged with their incessant chatter. Some kids can't stop moving. Other kids seem locked in an eternal slumber.

The beauty of focusing on the right relationship rather than doing the right things is that it can be applied in every family, whether you bring in a six-figure income or live just above the poverty line. In fact, abundant resources can be very dangerous. They can skew what really matters and turn a well-meaning parent into a human ATM. Let's look at the issue of "things" and parenting, and then we'll discuss basic principles (*not* how to's) of being a good parent.

Giving Kids What You Have

Dr. Benjamin Carson, a renowned surgeon at Johns Hopkins, tells a moving story about his mother. Mrs. Carson insisted that Ben and his brother Curtis write a book report every couple of weeks. This wasn't for school—this was for their mom.

Ben and Curtis dutifully obeyed.

About the time he was in junior high, Ben finally realized something quite shocking. *His mom couldn't read.* For years Ben had read books and scratched out reports, assuming that his mom was checking every word. But she didn't have a clue what he was saying.

Now consider this: Raised by an illiterate mother, Ben grew up to be a world-famous surgeon who was featured in many articles and was the author of several books. His illiterate mom didn't twist her hands over her lack of learning and give up hope of raising intelligent boys. Instead, she gave her boys what she had—interest, accountability, and the courage to demand extra work.

And it paid off.

Years later, someone asked Ben why his mother still lived with him, even after he was married and had a family of his own. "You don't understand," Ben answered. "If it weren't for that woman, I wouldn't be living here. She's earned this."

You could keep yourself awake every night by thinking about what you're not able to give your child, or what you lack as a parent. But you can give your child only what you have. I had to be reminded of this myself. Remember back when Sande told me that I was about to become a father again—at the age of forty-nine? I went into a full-fledged funk. I felt more sorry for the developing child than I did for me.

When she gets in high school and finds out how old we are, she's gonna sue us! I remember thinking. In all seriousness, I grieved, realizing that I probably wouldn't be there for much of her children's—my grandchildren's—lives. *Lauren had better marry a guy with a young father if she wants her kids to know what a grandpa's hugs feel like,* I thought.

And then we weren't sure how Lauren would turn out. When a woman is pregnant at forty-seven, doctors afflict you with the knowledge of every possible malady that can lay siege to the baby of a middle-aged woman.

In short, we just didn't feel like we had much to give a baby.

Then I went on a business trip to New York and stopped off to see a good childhood friend I call Moonhead and his wife, Wendy. As I lamented about Sande's pregnancy—how old we were, how risky it was for the developing child, how in many ways it was so unfair to her— Wendy just about knocked me over with a simple question.

"Can you think of a better family for that little girl to be born in?" she asked.

It was like somebody turned a light on, one of those *Aha!* moments that make everything clear. We do, indeed, have a very close family. We love one another very much. And I felt confident that Lauren's older sisters and brother would willingly play surrogate grandparents to their youngest sister's children, should the need arise.

We couldn't give Lauren parents who were in their twenties or thirties. We couldn't promise we'd be there for her when she hits her sixties. But Wendy helped me see there was much we could give to her—a loving home, a stable family, a truckload of care—and reminded me that I should focus on that.

Rather than stew over what they lack, good parents give their kids what they have—and then they strategically remember that what they *don't* give their children is also important.

What You Don't Give Your Children

When I come home from a trip, you won't find my suitcase filled with presents. I give my kids *me*, not toys. I want the focus of my return to be on renewing our relationship, not on some trinket that will take them away from me just as I arrive home.

Think about it. Why would a father who has been gone for several days want to give his children anything that they'll want to go off and play with now that he's finally back?

Sometimes, I'll come across something on the road that fits one of my children unusually well. Maybe it's something they've been looking for, or it's a present that when I see it I think, *That would be perfect for so-and-so.* In these cases, I will go ahead and buy it, because it's a present that is based on relationship, not guilt or obligation. When my daughter receives that present, she'll know I got it because I *know* her. Nobody else could have picked out that present, and because of that, the gift reinforces our relationship.

Getting an indiscriminate toy just because you need to get *something* is one of the more damaging things you can do! It demeans our daughters—as if we can buy them off—and adds an element of insincerity into our relationship.

Your kids don't need the material things you didn't have as a kid. Not giving kids things is very important. Earlier in this century, when the economy wasn't so strong and large families were much more common, many kids learned to do without—and they turned out very well. When I meet people who are later-borns in large families, I like to kid them, "I bet you were in junior high before you found out that chicken noodle soup has chicken *and* noodles, weren't you?"

My father grew up in an Irish immigrant family that had as its motto, "The first one up is the best dressed." If you slept in, there was no telling what you'd end up wearing that day.

Yet these families did fine because they drank their fulfillment from the soul-satisfying waters of relationship rather than wringing out a few bitter drops from consumerism.

You can make a powerful statement to your children by thinking carefully about what you shouldn't give them. Parenting isn't about being Santa Claus; it's about building a relationship.

If kids don't need that much in the way of things, what do they need relationally? Again, we can't provide "five easy steps" to become a good father, but we can look at some characteristics of what makes a good father.

A Good Father's Profile

What makes a good father? There are a few characteristics that make a good father do his best to stand out from the rest.

A Father Who Is There

If you ask my daughters what they remember most about growing up in my house, they'll talk about Huggy Hairy and the Big Bad Wolf.

One of our favorite games was for me to pretend I was a ferocious wolf. I chased Krissy and Holly around the room, "captured" them, then put them in the "pot" (on the couch) to cook them. I sprinkled them with invisible salt, put in a few imaginary vegetables, but always forgot the pepper.

"Oh no!" I'd say out loud. "I forgot the pepper!"

That was their cue. They knew I'd turn my back, and then they could "escape." At which, of course, I'd moan and groan as if I could never have foreseen such an occurrence if I lived to be a thousand years old.

To play Huggy Hairy, I turned out all the lights, lit a candle, and walked slowly down the hall. The closer I got, my shadow grew longer, and the girls were as terrified as they were delighted, huddling under the covers, occasionally taking a tantalizing peek to see how close Huggy Hairy was getting.

"It wasn't the organized activities that I remember," Holly says, "but the spontaneous fun, the Huggy Hairy moments, that stand out for me."

I didn't follow a rule book; I was just there, and that meant as much to my daughters as anything else I've ever done.

A classic study was done to determine if kids behave better on playgrounds with fences or without fences. The results were clear: Kids on playgrounds felt less secure and used less of the play yard when there was no fence. They huddled in the middle, and only a very few were brave enough to venture out and use the outside area of the yard. What some psychologists thought was demeaning ("You're caging them in like animals"), kids found comforting.

The parameters of life really help children. Having a dad present and active in the home is like having a fence on a playground. His presence provides assurance and comfort and makes a huge difference.

That's why I stress that kids need to have dinner with their family—including the father—most nights of the week. Only routine, quality, and regularity can build a healthy sense of belonging. The daddy who makes sacrifices in the name of relationship will be rewarded. The man who passes up the position that will bolster his income by twelve thousand dollars a year but send him out on the road for weeks at a time (I pass up many speaking engagements a year), the man who makes the choice to put relationship above everything else and who chooses to be present in the home, will make a profound difference in the lives of his children, especially his daughters.

That's why I don't listen to my kids when they say, "Please, Dad, don't show up for my game. You yell too much and embarrass me."

Krissy said that to me once and tried to back it up by saying, "Besides, it's an away game, almost two hours away."

She went on about how it's "not cool" to have your dad come and watch your game—or worse, to cheer for you from the stands.

Even so, I suspect she knew me well enough to know that if she was on a court, I'd be in the stands. I walked into the gym just before the volleyball game got started and saw Krissy lift her pinkie on her left hand, which was resting on her knee. That's all the greeting she would give me, physically, but her eyes and the light in her face said all I needed to know. She really did want me there.

This sense of a father's presence and support—particularly with athletics—is even more important for girls. Dr. Michael Nelson, chair of the American Academy of Pediatrics' Committee on Sports Medicine and Fitness, said, "The single most important factor in encouraging girls' participation in sports is parental role modeling."[1]

Lynn Jaffee, program coordinator at the Melpomene Institute of Women's Health Research in St. Paul, Minnesota, believes that a father's involvement is crucial because society in general doesn't pay much attention to female sports. "While women skiers, figure skaters, divers, and gymnasts earn some media coverage, women's sports teams receive no attention," she told the Health and Fitness News Service. "And except for a tiny handful of women tennis and golf pros, there's almost no money down the road for girls who play sports."[2]

The danger of this is not that athletically gifted women can't earn the money of a Michael Jordan, but that young girls may be less inclined to participate in sports activities, which are very healthy and which promote good character. Since society doesn't reinforce this—focusing more on Cindy Crawford and other supermodels rather than active, athletic women—without a father's interest, a daughter may lack the motivation and reinforcement to take part in team-oriented athletics.

Showing up when your daughter is on the court tells her more than that you value her physical health, however. It also speaks loudly about how much you value her: "You're important. You matter. What interests you interests me." She knows what a demanding schedule you have, and your willingness to put your own life aside to enter her life literally forms her soul. If the principal male in a young woman's life affirms her this way, it will shape her expectations and present a rather formidable defense against the jerks and takers who view women only as sex objects or servants.

A friend of mine, professional golfer Don Pooley, affirmed his daughter in a dramatic way. He took four months off the tour in 1998 just so he could watch his daughter's basketball team win their second consecutive 1-A Arizona State championship.

Pooley told the *Arizona Daily Star*, "I try to be there for everything important in [my kids'] lives. It's not going to matter if I play another golf tournament. I've played hundreds of golf tournaments. It's not going to matter if I miss a golf tournament; but it will matter if I miss something important to them."

Kerri was so touched by the sacrifice her father made—dropping off a professional tour to watch a girls' high school team—that she gave her best, and was named to the all-tournament team. Interestingly enough, Don came back from his four-month hiatus and made headlines by winning the Touchstone Energy Tucson Open Shootout.[3]

Our family has developed a tradition in which every Christmas Eve finds all the kids sleeping together in the same room. One year we were in a house in New York that didn't have a bedroom large enough to accommodate all of us, so we slept in a long hallway. The kids were delighted.

Father-affirmation isn't accomplished in one big moment. Relationship isn't a seamless concrete highway; it's more like a gravel walkway, built by adding one tiny stone after another, one little deposit of time, one gesture of concern, one offering of empathy.

Girls need a father who is there. (I'd like to coin a new adage: A man's place is in the home.) They also need a father who understands.

A *Father Who Understands*

One time at breakfast, Holly was emoting, as adolescents are known to do, and super-psychologist dad jumped in with the clear solution. It was so obvious I couldn't believe she had missed it.

After I spewed my wisdom all over her cornflakes, I waited for the family's applause. Instead, I was greeted by a molten silence that practically curdled the milk in my cocoa.

"Dad, you know what you ought to do?" Holly finally offered.

"What's that?"

"You ought to read your own books."

Whoosh!

I had been the typical father, running over Holly emotionally, not taking the time to enter her world but rather dancing on top of it like a benevolent dictator. I assumed I knew what I was talking about, but I didn't, and I ran over her feelings in the process.

"Holly, I'm sorry. I was wrong."

Man, did she nail me! She went for the jugular and she hit it, dead-center. I was two hundred and twenty-five pounds of oatmeal for the next three hours.

Dad, don't try to *fix* your daughter. *Relate* to her. Get to know her. Stop trying to solve your daughter's problems. She doesn't want you to fix anything. She just wants you to understand.

Understanding requires something infinitely more difficult than fixing. Understanding means I have to put down what I'm doing long enough to enter my daughter's world. Instead of racing to a conclusion with the answer, I need to be willing to travel with her in her uncertainty. She wants me to focus on the *process* while every testosterone-laden bone in my body is screaming for me to get to the *conclusion*.

What I need to say is not, "Honey, the answer is simple . . ." Instead, I need to show empathy. "Honey, you really seem bothered by this. Why don't you tell me about it?"

Unfortunately I've not always understood my daughter's feelings as well as I should have. Once, when Holly was sixteen, she brought her new boyfriend to the house to meet us. As she was introducing me to this young man, I realized that my shirt was hanging out. Not wanting to look disheveled for this important person in my daughter's life, I decided to try to alleviate the problem. Carefully, rather secretly, I thought, I unbuttoned the pants button and zipped down the fly. The next steps were not so inconspicuous, but hey, the boy and I shared the same anatomy. I opened my pants, felt around to find the shirttail, and tucked the sucker in. I did all this while I was saying, "Hi, nice to meet you." Then I shook the kid's hand.

To me, it was just one of those little things. Not to Holly. She was just dying. Unfortunately I've done lots of things like that over the years.

If a father will simply show some interest in his daughter's concerns and problems, he'll pass on to her an inheritance that even Bill Gates couldn't buy.

A daughter also needs a father who honors his wife.

A *Father Who Honors His Wife*

I'm not talking about genuflecting before your spouse here. I'm talking about something much more practical.

For instance, imagine a typical evening in which everyone is going in five different directions, and the house is left in disarray. The wife is out late, and on the way home she remembers how the kitchen looked when she left it. *As dead tired as I am*, she says to herself, *I'm gonna clean those dishes. I can't bear to wake up in the morning with that mess lying downstairs.*

Now it's a biological fact that most men are quite capable of sleeping as soundly as a bear in hibernation when there are enough dishes in the sink to service a platoon of soldiers. It's also well known that estrogen and dirty dishes don't mix. Nine out of ten women can't get their eyes closed if the kitchen isn't tidy.

So husband gets home forty-five minutes before the wife. Instead of getting a bowl of ice cream and watching *Sportscenter*, he opts to actually clean the kitchen. Not just stack the dirty dishes in the sink, mind you, but *actually put them in the dishwasher*. He might even really break the mold and wash the counters too.

The wife walks in, wearing the burden of her future chores like a heavy coat, but does a double take when she sees shine where she expected grime. She walks back outside to check the number on the house and is filled with all sorts of elation when she realizes that yes, this is her house, and no, she hasn't walked in on somebody else's husband.

That's the type of honoring I'm talking about.

Let me put it another way. How would you feel if you watched your young daughter suddenly grow twenty years in twenty minutes and you were allowed to peek in on her marriage? You watch as your tired little thirty-five-year-old comes home from running Johnny, Susie, and Katie all over town and is greeted by a husband who's getting more potato chips on the couch than he is in his mouth. The sink is piled with dishes, the carpet has enough dirt to create a pitcher's mound for Yankee stadium, and the husband is bellowing about being hungry.

Is this the environment you want your daughter to live in for the last fifty or sixty years of her life?

Your little girl will develop her expectations for her husband by watching how you treat her mother. If you act like a controlling, demanding, and lazy bum, your daughter won't think it odd or undesirable when she dates a boy who treats her this way. The best thing you can do to shape your daughter's view of men is to treat your wife like you want your future son-in-law to treat your daughter. More often than not, it will become a self-fulfilling example.

Daughters and sons need to see that Daddy treats Mommy as someone special. That tells daughters that they are worthy of respect. That tells sons that certain activities are inappropriate. I may be slow with some things, but I'm laser quick when it comes to my kids mouthing off to their mom. "Don't you *ever* think you can get away with talking to your mother like that," I say. I want to preserve Mom's place of honor.

A daughter needs a father who is there, a father who understands, a father who honors his wife, and a father who believes in her.

A Father Who Believes in His Daughter

Over forty years ago, a young woman named Elizabeth wanted to do something no girl had ever done in her hometown: She decided to run for the presidency of her high school.

"My father believed in me," Elizabeth explained in 1992, talking to a *Good Housekeeping* reporter. "I grew up feeling respected."

Not only did John Van Hanford, Elizabeth's dad, instill in his daughter the belief that she could achieve great things, but his fathering was such that Elizabeth found it easy to relate to men. "I grew up liking men because I liked my father, and it was apparent he liked himself."

Given this, it's not surprising that Elizabeth made a wise choice for a husband—a man who served for years as a respected senator from Kansas and then presidential nominee from the Republican Party. "What I admire and respect [in my husband] is what I admired and respected in my dad," Elizabeth explained.[4]

Some of you may have guessed what I'm about to tell you. Elizabeth married a man by the name of Robert Dole. She went on to become Secretary of Transportation under the Reagan administration, and until recently served as director of the American Red Cross.

Today, virtually all restrictions are off women. As I write this, two women sit on the Supreme Court. We have a female Secretary of State. Women run businesses, participate in their own professional basketball league, win the World's Cup in soccer, and even hold high positions in the military.

A father can encourage his daughter with more sincerity today than ever before, because there are very few things a woman can't do. If she wants to be a pilot, she can be a pilot. If she wants to be a CEO, she can be a CEO.

In just one week in the summer of 1999 two different publications featured two women who have broken the glass ceiling: Carole Black, CEO of the Lifetime cable network, and Carly Fiorina, CEO of

Hewlett-Packard. Both women replaced male CEOs. And both women have extensive backgrounds in business. Black rose to vice president of marketing and TV at Walt Disney and was also general manager of NBC's TV station in Los Angeles. Fiorina is credited with orchestrating Lucent Technologies' 1996 spinoff from AT&T.

Yet I'm not sure I agree with Carly Fiorina who said, "I hope that we are at a point that everyone has figured out that there is not a glass ceiling."[5]

The same news article cited this fact: In the entire Fortune 500, only two other companies are headed by women, and females make up only 11 percent of senior executives.[6]

Even though the glass ceiling may be only cracked, dads need to realize that girls have as much a chance to fulfill their dreams as boys.

For fathers who place family first, there may be some reluctance to encourage their daughters in this, as many would like to see their girls actually raise their children rather than drop them off at the kiddy kennel. That's something with which I wholeheartedly agree. But fathers can play a major role in helping their daughters understand the reality of the workplace. Since you've been there, you can help her figure out how she can fit into a vocation without sacrificing her family.

For example, you can encourage her to delay childbearing until she and her husband have the financial means to keep one parent at home once the kids arrive. You can point out to her what the research is clearly finding: Women are leaving large, corporate businesses in droves and going into business for themselves. This gives women the freedom to fulfill family obligations while still helping out with the family budget.

As fathers, we can prepare our daughters so that they don't have to choose between vocational success and letting someone else raise their children. We know how the world works and can rely on that experience to help our daughters explore a family-friendly way to earn money. To do this, we have to believe in them and be involved in their lives. We also have to be convinced that our daughters really do have something to offer the world.

Mail order, the Internet, and telecommuting are changing the face of corporate America. The old way of doing business may bear little resemblance to the future. One thing that hasn't changed—and won't change—is that women want freedom of time more than anything else. A good dad will help his daughter understand that real wealth is measured by owning your own schedule, not by owning three homes.

The first and most important step in this is simply doing what John Van Hanford did for Elizabeth: Believe in your daughter. Don't cultivate dreams for your sons and give your daughters the leftovers.

Finally, a daughter needs a father who lets her get hurt.

A Father Who Lets His Daughter Hurt

As a teenager, Holly went through some terrible operations on her jaw to alleviate TMJ dysfunction (temporomandibular joint, which is a very long word for excruciating pain in the jaw joints, pain that doesn't cease); horrific would not be too dramatic a description. She missed weeks and weeks of school, most of her high school years, in fact. Even so, she graduated near the top of her class.

At one point she told me she wanted to give the doctors one more try. "No way!" I said as firmly as I could. "They've hurt you enough."

The failure rate had been so high and Holly's suffering had been so great, I just couldn't bear to see my daughter go under the knife again.

"Dad," she pled with me, "I don't want to deal with this pain for the rest of my life. It'll hurt a bit more in the short run, but I have to give it one more try."

I was skeptical, but with Sande's urging I finally relented. The operation wasn't a complete success, but it did make things much better. I was wrong in opposing the operation; I was so blinded by the short-term pain Holly would feel, it was difficult to see the long-term gain.

The hardest thing a father can do is let his daughter hurt, but sometimes pain is the only path to maturity. For some reason most fathers recognize the need to toughen sons by letting them hurt. If a boy comes home with a bloody nose, our natural reaction is, "Here, let me tell you how to hit him back." If our daughter comes home with a bloody nose, we start thinking about the bazooka in the back of our closet.

This is a tough world. In many ways, it's tougher on women than it is on men. As we raise our daughters, we must be careful we don't stunt their maturity by acting as if pain has nothing to teach them. Just because your daughter is struggling doesn't mean that you as a good father should rush in to save her. Sometimes being a good father means letting your daughter work her own way out of a tight and even painful spot. I'm not suggesting this is easy—it may be the toughest thing you ever do—but it's essential.

That's why I consciously use pain—including negative emotions— to help my daughters mature. By now you know I'm a big proponent of using affirmation and encouragement in liberal doses, but that doesn't exclude using painful emotions as well.

Our two youngest girls now routinely empty the dishwasher. Hannah puts away the dishes while Lauren, who is much shorter, puts away the silverware. One evening, Hannah obviously wasn't feeling well. She could barely sit up at the dinner table, so afterward we said, "Go ahead and lie down, Hannah. You don't have to do any work tonight."

Then followed something we hate to hear in the Leman house—whining from Lauren. Lauren is the type of kid who, if you told her to dig a well in the backyard, she would immediately pick up a shovel and begin digging. But something got into her that night, and she started in with a refrain that every parent has heard one time or another: "That's not fair. Why does Hannah get off? How come *I* have to do all the work?"

I finally stepped back into the kitchen and said, "Lauren, why don't you go to your room? You don't have to do the dishes tonight. Daddy will do your work for you."

Her face fell ten feet, which is quite an accomplishment, given the fact that she's less than four feet tall. Twenty seconds later, she was back in the kitchen. "I'll do the dishes, Daddy."

"No, Lauren, you go back to your room. Daddy is doing your work."

I chose my words carefully. *Daddy* is doing *your* work. There wasn't a worse punishment I could give a girl like Lauren. She felt incredibly guilty, and I *wanted* her to feel guilty. We squashed that whining bug right then and there.

To raise responsible daughters, it is sometimes necessary to use negative emotions. I spend many hours ruminating on how to make Lauren and Hannah feel accepted, loved, and affirmed. But when the time is right, I'm not afraid to let them feel hurt, guilty, or even ashamed. I'm definitely a "grace" person more than a "law" person, but there is a time in every family's life where a sting is essential to introduce a child to reality.

I had barely put the last dish away when Lauren came out again, looking like a lost soul. She wanted to approach me, but she didn't know how, so she took these tiny steps, looking up at me after each one to make sure I wasn't going to gobble her up.

"I'm sorry I didn't do the dishes," she said.

"Do you understand why Daddy was upset?"

"Yes."

"When Mommy and Daddy ask you to do something around the house, we expect you to do it with what kind of face?"

"A happy face."

"What kind of face did you have?"

"A pouting face."

I loved her, gave her a kiss, affirmed her, but reinforced the lesson. She hurt, but she grew, and she hasn't whined about the dishes since.

A Good Dad

How much does it cost to "buy" the qualities of a good dad—being there, understanding your daughter, honoring your wife, believing in your girl, letting the daughter grow through pain?

Last time I checked, it was free.

How many degrees does it take to learn this esoteric formula?

The answer is easy. You don't have to go to school at all. Why? Being a good dad is about being relational. It's not what you can buy your kids; it's not slick strategies or secret lessons. It's taking time to be there, to care, to get involved. That's what a good dad is—relational.

He's there. He cares.

Don't worry about being a great dad. Just practice being a good one, and your daughters will be richly blessed.

CHAPTER 6
Make Waffles, Not Wafflers

Paul Harvey tells the true story of a young mother who watched her four-year-old daughter jump up from watching the television and run to her room. The daughter's actions were so sudden, the mother followed her child to find out what she was up to. She found her girl pulling clothes out of her closet.

"What are you doing?" she asked.

"Barney told me I could join his fan club if I sent him my name and a dress," the girl answered.

This is a confusing world for young children. A friend of mine has built a trail through the woods in the back of his house. At one point, he constructed some steps with a guardrail on an incline. He noticed that his four-year-old daughter always got very scared at this point in the trail. When she saw her little brother walking beside the steps instead of on them, she screamed out, "Watch out! The boys will get you!"

"What are you talking about?" the father asked.

"You told me I shouldn't walk off the steps because the boys in hiding are there."

The father laughed. "I said there's *poison ivy* there, not *boys in hiding*."

A science museum in the west has an exhibit that I wish every parent could sit in. They've constructed a chair and table that allows a six-foot adult to experience what it is like for a three-foot child in most homes. The giant set is built to scale, so a father can actually see how large everything seems to his little girl. His legs dangle from the chair, he sees how thick the table legs appear, and he has to get used to the fact that his chin barely clears the tabletop.

It's amazing, the feelings that being small engender. If you saw the movie *Honey, I Shrunk the Kids*, you might have a better idea of what I'm talking about.

The world is a big, scary, and confusing place. That's why I disagree wholeheartedly with those who say we should take our hands off and let kids find their own way. While I certainly believe we need to be sensitive about a child's temperament and natural bent, I also believe it is crucial that fathers take a conscious role in using that information to shape their children. Otherwise, our children will be lost, misled, and exploited.

Children who have not been imprinted positively have poor identities. They're wafflers. They'll become whatever they think someone wants them to become, just to fit in with their peers. Their life energy will be consumed with trying to look like what they think the world wants them to look like.

A young girl who has been lovingly, thoughtfully, and carefully imprinted by her father has been equipped to say no to a peer group that demands, "be like us." There is no better antidote to peer pressure than a father's affirmation.

A daughter can't get this affirmation from her pastor, Sunday school teacher, Girl Scout leader, or instructor at school. Parents these days are all too quick to drop their kids off at church, at school, at the doctor's office, and even at their counselor's office. Their attitude runs something like this: *You fix my kid while I read these magazines.*

The fact is, you have to be relevant in your kids' lives. It's not as important for the pastor or youth leader to be relevant as it is for the parent to be relevant. To be relevant means that the father intersects with his daughter and enters her life in a meaningful way.

This can be as simple as choosing a thoughtful gift for your daughter yourself rather than leaving such tasks to the mother. After Krissy was married, one of the things she remembered most clearly was that I signed many of her birthday cards instead of Sande.

Daughters notice these things.

On her thirteenth birthday, I went to a jewelry store and designed an amethyst ring for my second-born. To this day, Krissy still has it. Out of all the gifts she has received, this is one she remembers the most because it took initiative on my part to pick it out, design it, and purchase it.

I wanted the ring to be personal so that the act of giving it would positively imprint my daughter. As you get older, you realize you only get so many shots to do this imprinting. The day will come when your daughter's personality—and affections—are set. The wet cement of childhood will transform itself into the concrete form of an adult.

Imprinted children are waffles—they're the Shirli Hunts, mentioned earlier in this book, who have been so influenced by their parents they have adopted the morals, ideals, and priorities of their family as their own. They're set, sturdy, and ready to face the world with their own distinctive mark.

Success!

Book tours can be chaotic. You're in a town you're unfamiliar with, trying to find addresses on a tight schedule, frequently living in a time zone other than what your body is conditioned to, and eating whenever you get the chance.

It makes a world of difference to have a competent author escort, and on one occasion, I had the best. (The publisher hires these escorts. It's their job to get the author to the right place at the right time.)

The young woman I'm talking about seemed groomed for her position. She possessed a charming ability to put people—even frazzled radio station producers and tired authors—at ease, open the right doors, and handle the curve balls of a tour. This isn't as easy as it might sound. Interviews can be changed at the last minute, and this tends to create a domino effect. A good escort needs to be able to make on-the-spot judgments; sometimes, she'll have to choose to dump a smaller show in favor of a larger show. This particular escort handled herself with such class that everybody commented about how wonderful she was.

Over the three days I was in town, we talked about everything you could imagine. One thing she said surprised me as much as it pleased me. Keep in mind, this was a very competent single woman. She was attractive, vivacious, and captivating. Finding a marriage partner wouldn't be a problem, but guess what she told me? "I would never marry anyone my mother and father did not approve of."

You have to trust your parents a lot to make that kind of statement.

Some might even see this as a weakness, but I don't look at it that way. What it tells me is that she's been properly imprinted—she's a waffle, not a waffler—with many good skills and talents, but the wisdom to know she still needs her parents' input.

I realized she didn't become her competent self by accident or neglect; her parents took the time to affirm her and help build the confidence and self-esteem she needed to do her job well as an adult.

I honestly believe we have just two choices. Somebody is going to shape our child—either us or the world. As a parent, I believe God gives that responsibility to me. There is no way I can shield my children from the ugly realities of life, even if I wanted to. But what I can do is use those ugly realities to teach valuable lessons.

That's what I did with Krissy one day at the supermarket.

Negative Imprinting

"Daddy, do something!"

Krissy was frantic. We were standing across a shopping center parking lot and saw a man slap a woman in the face and then shove her into a car. They were off before I could reach them.

I turned to Krissy and said, "Krissy, I'm sorry you had to see that, but you need to know something. There are men in this world who treat their wives like that all the time. They abuse women and hurt them."

I waited to let these words sink in. I wanted her to be sobered so that my next words would be even more effective.

"Your job is to find a man who treats you with respect. Your mission is to find a man who will honor you and care for you and *never* hit you."

I could see Krissy's brain working on overdrive to process all that she had seen and heard. Fathers must warn women of the dangers they face in life. There are some of the sickest predatory creatures out there known to humankind. As we imprint our daughters, we must guide them to what is best.

So often when my kids were growing up, we'd drive by an accident, flares lighting up the sky, a car rolled over, ambulance and police personnel milling about, and always I would say out loud, "Drugs or alcohol. I bet this had to do with drugs." Before too long my kids would speak up before I did. When we came up on an accident, one of them would say, "Think it was a druggie, Dad?" They were ingrained to connect drugs and alcohol with accidents.

I want to put positive imprints on my kids, but it's just as important that I put negative imprints on them. I want my children to associate the positive things in life—respect, vocational success, stability, and the like—with the positive virtues of morality, hard work, and loyalty. And I want them to associate the negative things in life—tragedy, financial ruin, upheaval—with the things that usually cause them—irresponsibility, laziness, selfishness.

Tragedy occasionally strikes good and decent people. But it is *certain* to follow foolishness. It's only a matter of time. If a daughter marries a violent man, eventually, she will be hit.

This is the travesty of silent fathers. Daughters look to their fathers to determine how the world works. When the father doesn't actively tell them, they are forced to make a guess and find their own way. Try to remember how little you knew about the world as it really was when you were eighteen years old. Do you want your daughter making decisions now with no more knowledge than you had then?

Imprinting is only partially about what we say. It is even more influenced by what we do. Dad, what does your daughter see when she observes you with your wife? Does she see love, kindness, consideration, and a willingness to serve? Or does she see competition, cheap shots, or even physical or psychological abuse? If your little girl wrote an essay on how a husband should treat his wife based solely on what she has seen under your roof, what would that essay say?

Take Your Daughter to a Funeral

I'm all for taking daughters to church, but an occasional funeral can be just as helpful.

A friend of mine made a special point of taking his three children to a funeral for a young man who died of AIDS. The young man contracted the HIV virus through using drugs, and he consequently died in prison. He was in his early thirties, without a wife, without children, slowly languishing in a prison cell. He died a slow and painful death, lapsing in and out of consciousness before he finally breathed his last.

On the way to the funeral, this father said, "Kids, I want you to see what you're really missing when someone tries to turn you on to drugs. Do you want to die alone in a prison cell when you're still young? Do you want to experience having a body that has been ravished by a violent disease? Do you want your last image of this world to be the four walls of a prison cell? Is that the legacy you want to leave behind?"

This is a very positive form of negative imprinting. Don't be silent when you read the newspaper. When you come across an article about the latest college frat boy who drank himself to death with alcohol poisoning, point it out to your daughter. "This is what happens every year," you can remind her. "Drinking large quantities of alcohol can kill you."

I know you're busy, Dad. We all are. But there are simply too many voices clamoring for our daughters' attention for us to remain silent.

So Many Voices

When Hannah was seven years old, she had a toy computer that talked to her. It used simple, prerecorded language: "Welcome. Please select a category now."

One time, two-year-old Lauren pulled the computer between her legs and turned it on.

This is gonna be good, I thought to myself.

"Welcome," the computer said. "Please select a category now."

Lauren didn't know what to do, so she just sat there. After fifteen seconds or so, the computer spoke up again. "Please select a category now."

Lauren let slip an exasperated sigh, cupped her hands around her mouth, bent down toward the computer, and called out, "Lady, I'm only two years old."

Voices are calling out to our children night and day—teen magazines, talk shows, teachers who abide by different life values, entertainers who become famous by flaunting their immorality. Kids left on their own simply don't have the experience and maturity to adequately filter these voices.

That's where Dad needs to step up. Give your children an opportunity through your counsel to benefit from your wisdom and avoid many of the mistakes you may have made in life. Otherwise, by your silence, you force your kids to walk blindly through life. They'll have to guess what road is best without the benefit of a father's understanding.

Every day voices are screaming. One silent day from dad might be the one day that your daughter accepts a lie as truth. "This isn't sex; this is just 'touching.'" "This isn't really a drug. It's natural. It grows out of the ground."

On the other hand, if you take the time to imprint your daughter when she's young, you'll save both you and her a lot of heartache in the future.

Shortly after she moved away to college, Krissy wrote her mom a letter. I won't share the entire epistle, but two paragraphs in particular show the value of making waffles instead of wafflers.

I now realize the wisdom that you and Dad have. When I was younger I never understood that. Now I do. You and Dad have taught me so much. If it wasn't for your guidance and love and discipline, I would never make it here at college. The morals you have taught me are now the characteristics that I cling to. Especially now that I'm on my own.

Thank you for taking time to love me and teach me in a Christian manner. I hope that one day, I'll be as good a mom as you are. I miss my family so much. I'm realizing that friends come and go—but my family will always be there.

Can't wait till Christmas!

Love,
Kristin Sarah
XOXOXOXO

The words that touch me the most are these: *"The morals you have taught me are now the characteristics that I cling to. Especially now that I'm on my own.*" That's what imprinting is all about—training up a child in the way she should go (according to her bent), and then finding out that when she is grown, she has internalized those same values and chooses to live by them.

CHAPTER 7
Miss Trust

"For fifty bucks you could have saved yourself a whole lot of trouble."

You know it's going to be a long day when you start it being lectured by a flight attendant.

Here's the story: It was the end of the summer, and Hannah needed to fly from our summer home in New York State to Tucson, Arizona, where we spend the school year. She wanted to spend a week with her friend there before the rest of our family moved back home to Tucson. I didn't want nine-year-old Hannah to fly alone, so I decided to accompany her. I reserved a round-trip ticket that had me flying back to Buffalo forty-five minutes after Hannah and I arrived in Tucson.

When the flight attendant found out what I was doing—spending an entire day flying from Buffalo to Tucson and then immediately back to Buffalo, just to chaperone my daughter—she couldn't believe it.

"Why didn't you just put her on the plane?" she asked. "We chaperone kids much younger than her all the time. Don't you trust us? We do a good job."

"It's not your job," I replied. "It's mine."

Her mouth dropped. She literally did not know what to say. Before the flight was over, I had several attendants gathered around to talk to this crazy man who insisted on flying with his daughter.

I take the protective role of parenting very seriously. Just recently, I read in the paper how one mother was furious at an airline for putting her six-year-old son in a hotel room with a fifteen-year-old boy. The plane had been delayed by weather, so the airline was forced to find a room for everyone. To save money, they asked the two boys to stay in the same room. According to the mom, the older boy molested her son.

While I understand the mother's anguish, I'm also curious as to why she thought her six-year-old son was mature enough to travel on his own. Flights are frequently disrupted, rerouted, or canceled, and I find it hard to believe so many parents casually send such young children unattended on cross-country flights.

I honor protective parents, even when it pinches my own feet. I really admire one father, in large part because he refused to let me date his daughter in high school. (I think that shows he had a good bit of insight!)

The dad's friend was the school superintendent, very well respected, a distinctive dresser (always wore bow ties), the type who would show up for the symphony performance or serve on the art council. This friend took my would-be girlfriend's father aside and said, "You really shouldn't let your daughter date this Leman kid. He's a terrible student and not a good person."

He was half right. I *was* a terrible student, but I don't think I was a bad person. Nevertheless, I admire fathers who step in and protect their daughters. Even if they occasionally misjudge a well-meaning teen—I was written off my entire adolescence—their approach is preferable to fathers who provide no guidance or protection or who are too busy to care.

When we protect our daughters, even though they may at times resent it, we are building a crucial element of their personality: *trust.*

You can divide most women into two camps. One camp is Miss Trust. The other is Mistrust. That one *s* makes all the difference in the world. The extra *s* is provided by the father, and it creates one of the richest inheritances that a son-in-law can receive from his wife's father.

If I could turn back the clock so that my six-year-old daughter Lauren were once again just two years old, I could perform an experiment that would make my wife cringe but would make a strong point to the audience. Let's say I called Lauren up on stage and told her to start climbing up a twenty-foot ladder—not all the way, just five or six feet. If I then told her to jump into my arms, she would have done it without hesitation.

I could then have put her up several rungs higher. Let's say she's now ten feet in the air. "Come on, honey," I might say, "jump into Daddy's arms." Without even thinking about it, she would have done a free fall—and Sande would immediately get rid of every ladder we owned.

Even as a two-year-old, Lauren trusted me thoroughly. She knew I wouldn't do anything to harm her, and that if I said I would catch her, I would. That's how much a little girl trusts her daddy.

I wish I could let you men in on some of my counseling sessions so you could see for yourself what happens when a woman lives with mistrust. Some women climbed that "ladder," and when they jumped, their fathers pulled back and let their daughters fall. Maybe the little girl remembers how her dad patted her on the head when she was six years old and promised her that even though he and her mother were getting a divorce, he'd call her three times a week—and broke his promise within the first seven days. Maybe her dad continually promised he'd take her shopping "tomorrow," but never followed through. Perhaps he told her he was "on the wagon"—and then came staggering home, his breath reeking of alcohol.

Quite understandably, these women often harbor a deep fury. The primary person in their life, the one they thought they could (and should have been able to) trust more than anyone else, let them down. As a consequence, these women often struggle with issues of trust throughout their lives.

A father who is trustworthy, who never lies, who follows through on his promises and can be counted on, turns mistrust into Miss Trust.

The marital marks of Miss Trust are these: She is going to be free and spontaneous and an equal partner in her marriage. She won't be afraid to tell her husband about what is really going on inside her. She won't run from vulnerability; rather, she'll embrace it. This is key, because any good psychologist will tell you that communication is vital to a fulfilling marriage—and good communication skills require a willingness to be vulnerable.

In so many ways, trust sets up a woman to become a true partner to her husband. A woman who is afraid to be vulnerable, who just can't trust men, is a woman who will draw back from her husband. To the degree she does that, her husband will be frustrated. He'll feel that he's not enough for her. He'll sense that she doesn't trust him. He'll feel cheapened, unworthy, and put down. That's a prescription for creating an unfaithful husband or a very short marriage.

Even worse, a father who doesn't consciously build trust in his daughter sets her up to be exploited by predatory men or boys.

Mistrust: Ready to Be Exploited

An experienced director of a crisis pregnancy center is finding that a growing number of young women don't even know what they're feeling.

"I know I've hit the right word when I see the tears come out," she says. She's learned she has to help young women understand their emotions by getting them to describe what's going on inside and then to find a label for it.

Unfortunately, one thing that has changed since she's begun counseling is that young women seem much less able to recognize feelings of abandonment.

A young man has gotten a young teenager pregnant and left her hanging in the lurch, but the girl doesn't understand the "funny" feelings inside. "He *loves* me," the client insists while the director and her counselors try not to shake their heads.

How can it be love when a boy runs at the first sign of trouble and leaves his girlfriend alone just when she's feeling vulnerable and afraid for the future?

It's my belief that these young women confuse abandonment and love because that's how their dads "loved" them. They want to believe their dads cared for them, even if their fathers were distant. This has radically distorted their filters. They don't expect loyalty; they don't see that trust is a vital part of a relationship. As long as they *feel* like they're in love, or as long as a boy *tells* a girl he loves her, she is convinced the love is genuine.

A father who fails to build trust in his daughter and who neglects to model loyalty and trustworthiness sets up his girl to be exploited by any number of men. Regardless of how she learns to cope, the mistrust sown in her life by her daddy will always play harmony to the daughter's frantic melody.

This phenomenon reminds me of one of those new "miracle sticks" that you use to repair small rips in fabric. You don't have to use a needle or thread anymore; just rub the stick over the tear and it's gone . . . until you hold it up to the light. Then you can clearly see the tear.

Some women are like that. There's been a tear in their life, but on the outside everything seems fixed. "This is the day the Lord has made, let us rejoice and be glad in it," one woman will say, but as soon as her life gets a little choppy, she panics. There's no bedrock of trust for her to lean on, no sense of security to envelop her. She acts like a terrified drowning victim who is likely to take others down with her.

She might not realize what is happening. She may not even connect her little peccadilloes with her fear of vulnerability, but that's what it is. "Okay, we can have sex, but it has to be in the dark, under the covers, on this side of the bed, with a towel underneath."

Even though this type of thinking is about as exciting to a man as shampooing a rug, he plays along because he senses that if he tries to pry into what's really going on, he'll wake up a bear—and he will.

A daughter who has learned to trust her dad will open up to her husband. Sex is by its nature a very vulnerable act. It's terrifying to many women, being naked and open to a man. If a female is dealing with trust issues, she'll have a hard time enjoying herself in marital intimacy.

Another one of the biggest hindrances to trust is a separated home. A daughter will naturally find it difficult to trust a man who has abandoned her mother.

Disneyland Dads

"I just want you to know, I've forgiven you, Dad."

"Forgiven me?" Frank asked. "For what? Spending all my vacations with you over the past ten years? Taking you to Disneyland and Washington, D.C.? Always paying for your support? Just which one of these things are you forgiving me for?"

Frank was surprised at the passion that spontaneously erupted within him. Clearly, his daughter was hitting a sore nerve.

"For abandoning me and Mom."

Frank heard himself gasp. He never expected this. His daughter Julie was now eighteen years old. She had figured out what had happened when Frank left his wife—Julie's mother—ten years prior, and remarried soon thereafter.

The surprising thing is, Frank was caught off guard. For some unfathomable reason, he thought his three kids would always have the understanding of a ten-, eight-, and six-year-old, respectively. It never occurred to him that his children would grow up and realize that regardless of the spin he put on why he left home, eventually they would reach their own conclusions.

Dads, I'm here to tell you, leaving home and then assuaging your guilt by taking your kids to Disneyland doesn't build trust. If anything, it undermines it. Here's why.

I can't tell you how many mothers have sat in my office, frustrated over the fact that it takes them two or three days to undo the damage that was done by their daughter's last visit with Dad. "For ten years, he worked fifty-five hours a week, spent Friday night shooting darts, and most of Saturday on the golf course," these mothers will tell me. "On Sunday, we could hardly pry him out of his recliner. Now all of a sudden he saves up his parenting for his twice-yearly trips. He runs the kids from morning to night, making them happy, happy, happy. They return home exhausted and wonder why life with me is so boring. For days, I notice a sharper tone in my daughter's answers, not to mention a bit of a sassy spin every time I ask her to do something."

Following a divorce, parents frequently compete for the child's attention. This doesn't build trust; it builds animosity—and it usually begins with the father using an unfair advantage. Typically, Mom has less money than Dad. There is no way she can compete with Dad's presents, Dad's trips, or Dad's shopping excursions. The mom will invariably shake her head as she listens to yet another account of twenty-four-hour fun: "The days were just packed!"

Trust is built when a daughter sees her mother *model* trust. If her parents are at war, a daughter learns to put up her guard. She sees her mom crying into her pillow. She hears her mom pouring out her heart to a friend, and she knows that somehow, *Daddy* is behind all this pain. There isn't a single place on earth a dad can take his daughter to help her forget her mother's pain.

Divorced moms and dads, can I talk to both of you for a moment? I know you couldn't agree on so much in the first place—that's why you got a divorce, after all—but how about sitting down and realizing that even after this divorce, for your daughter's sake, you need to get your acts together and come up with a game plan both of you can live with?

Ask yourselves, can we lay down the weapons for a few minutes and talk about what's best for our daughter? Can we come to an agreement that the basic rules that are part of our daughter's everyday life—such as bedtime, eating, and dating habits—will be basically reinforced in the other parent's home?

If you can agree to this, then at least the daughter won't see her mother greeting her after a daddy-visit with a face worn by apprehension. There won't be that trust-destroying interrogation: "How late were you out? Did he feed you right? You look so tired; are you sure you weren't up late?"

Even indirectly, when a mother goes through this ritual, she plants seeds of doubt in her daughter's soul that will grow into full-fledged mistrust. She's indirectly telling her, "Be wary of your father. He can't be trusted to do what's best for you. Visits with him are something we must tolerate, but fear."

Everybody loses under this scenario. The damage it does to a daughter's spirit, especially, is enduring.

Let's look now at how a father can nurture Miss Trust instead of mistrust.

Miss Trust: Ready to Experience Intimacy

My little six-year-old, Lauren, gets out of bed in the evening maybe once a year, so I knew when I saw her standing there that this wasn't an act of defiance. Something was wrong.

"Lauren, what's wrong, honey?" I asked.

"Daddy, there's a spider in my room and I'm scared."

We went back to her room, where I had just tucked her in moments before. Of course, I went through my rendition. "Little spiders won't hurt you, honey. It'll be okay. I know you're afraid, but you'll be okay."

"But, Daddy, what if he bites me?"

"Well, honey, listen. If you want to, you can sleep upstairs in the waterbed, though your little friends might miss you if you do that." Lauren has yet to meet a stuffed animal she doesn't adore, and she's surrounded by a plethora of critters every night.

My mentioning her plush playmates left Lauren in a quandary. I could see the gears turning in her little head—*Should I stay in my room with my friends and get eaten by a big ferocious spider? Or should I sleep elsewhere and risk offending my soft and very sensitive animals?*

Decisions don't get much tougher than this when you're three feet tall.

Lauren scraped her toes on the carpet, then looked up at me and said, "Daddy, if you were little like me, what would you do?"

"Well," I said, working up a tone that she could take confidence in, "if I were little tonight, I suppose I would sleep in the waterbed upstairs, knowing that Daddy will get the spider patrol after that spider and that he'll make sure the spider is not in your room tomorrow night."

Lauren sighed. Her decision was made; she'd sleep upstairs. The burden was lifted. She felt secure, knowing she could trust her dad.

Little moments like these are essential for a daughter to learn how to trust a man. This is where the basic thread of trust is sewn into the human personality. It's either there or it isn't, and you can't fake it.

That is one of the problems of being an absentee dad. You don't know when scary moments will arise in your daughter's life. If you live in a separate house or you're always at the office or out with the boys, your little daughter will learn to cope, but she'll never learn to trust a man and to be vulnerable.

Merely being home isn't enough, of course. Trust is often built in shared adventures. When she was still quite young, Krissy asked to go on a fishing trip with me, even though she had recently broken her arm.

We had to hike up to a cabin and cross a trout stream along the way. This wasn't a dangerous river, but it *was* a trout stream, so rapids were present, and Krissy was young. The water's movement pummeled her little legs. Krissy clung to me with an earnest hold. I looked in her face and saw the fear flooding her eyes, but a curious thing happened. She looked up at me, caught my eyes, and the fear dimmed. It wasn't erased, but there was a trusting sense of confidence behind it. I may not look like Tom Cruise, but at that moment Krissy didn't want to see a movie star. She wanted to see her dad.

These intangible moments shape a girl's soul in profound ways. When a daughter is afraid and learns that her dad is capable of leading her through her fear, later on she'll be confident that she and her husband can tackle life's fears together too.

In addition to facing your daughter's fears, a father builds trust by chasing out the chaos in his daughter's world.

Chaotic Kids

For those who watched *Saving Private Ryan*, you know that one of the most horrific aspects of war is its chaos. Storming the beaches of Normandy, American and British forces faced deadly force in all directions. German commander Erwin Rommel guarded Omaha Beach with crossing fire, plunging fire, and grazing fire. There was scarcely an inch of land that wasn't sighted by some type of German gun. American soldiers knew that if they stayed on the beach, they would certainly be killed. But to move forward meant exposing themselves to horrendous machine gun fire. It was a psychologically debilitating decision. Making a wrong choice carried the ultimate punishment— death. Yet doing nothing would exact the same price.

Though we live in peacetime, the world still seems a bit chaotic to our children. By bringing order to their world, we can help them build confidence and trust.

What many parents fail to realize is that kids often *know* they shouldn't be throwing tantrums. Inwardly, a child who is venturing into destructive or inappropriate behavior is frequently screaming, "Somebody help me get control of myself."

Even from a young age, Holly understood that my discipline had that aim. Disciplining her built trust: "Daddy will keep watch over me and rein me in if I ever get out of control." She now has the opportunity to bring that same control to other kids' lives.

The first year Holly taught, her students' parents often introduced themselves to me and invariably, within about three minutes, I'd hear the word *detention*. Holly's mother didn't raise any fools. If a kid came to school without being prepared, Holly made sure it didn't happen again by keeping them after school.

Over time, Holly learned how few kids have learned to control themselves. After she had been teaching a few years Holly told me, "It wasn't until I got around all these other families that I fully understood just how good I had it as a kid, and how good my own family was."

Holly learned order at home. She was trained to respect discipline, and now she spends her days trying to push back the chaos in other children's lives.

Men, if you want a challenge, think about what it means to overcome chaos with order: It means nothing less than living in the image of God. That's what God did, isn't it? He entered chaos—nothingness—and exerted His will, His purpose, and His creation.

Because God was able to do that, we have learned to trust Him. We are willing to stake our own salvation on His word because He has proven to us in our own lives that He is able to bring order to our chaos. We're called to do the same in our families.

We do this by bringing order into our homes. Instead of letting Mom do all the discipline, we step forward. We set limits to our kids' schedules, knowing that they'll fall apart and run themselves into the ground if we don't establish parameters. We provide as healthy an atmosphere as possible, living what we preach and sending a clear, uncompromised, and consistent message. What our daughters hear us say, they see us live; what they experience in church, they see modeled at home.

Living in a world of chaos, every little girl should be able to rest her soul at home. As fathers, we can give our daughters little places of refuge where they clearly understand what is expected of them. Men, such ordering doesn't happen by accident. A neglected business will ultimately fail. A yard left to itself will return to the wilderness. A family is no different. If the father doesn't establish order, he's inviting chaos.

Another way that a father builds trust in his daughter is by creating a healthy fear.

Healthy Fear

Recently, Krissy appeared on a radio show I cohost. My sidekick asked Krissy what it was like to grow up with me as a father, and one of the things Krissy mentioned was that she developed a "positive, not negative" fear of me. My cohost then asked me what is the difference between a positive and a negative fear.

A positive fear comes from this: When a father says something is going to happen, it happens. The daughter knows that certain behaviors will elicit a predictable response. This is scary if a daughter is contemplating misbehaving, but ultimately it's comforting for a daughter to know how her world works.

Dads, if you want to raise a Miss Trust instead of afflicting your daughter with mistrust, stick to your guns—but do this without shooting yourself in the foot. Be careful about backing yourself into a corner you can't get out of. When you lay down the law, you must be willing to abide by it. Otherwise, you'll let chaos creep into the corners of your family life.

Trust sinks its roots in *security* and *consistency*. When a daughter feels that the rules are always changing or that she can manipulate her way around her father's righteous wrath, it actually creates a climate of negative fear, because she realizes, "Everything depends on *me*. Unless I find a way to talk myself out of this, I'm doomed."

A consistent father provides security. The daughter knows that if she does A, B will result. There's no guesswork, and that is actually—in the end—more comforting. She learns to trust.

Another aspect of creating a healthy fear—in addition to being consistent—is being approachable. Even when we are rightfully angry, our daughters should know that we will never abuse them. They need the confidence that we can handle negative emotions without letting those feelings cascade into inappropriate behavior.

When Hannah was very young and just learning to write, she penned a short message after she got in trouble:

Dad, I ♥ u and hope your madness goes away. Tell me when it does because I kneed to ask you somthing.
♥ Hannah

Hannah knew I was angry, and she knew that she should probably let things cool off before we talked. But she also felt confident that the relationship was rock solid. She could look forward to the near future when we could communicate with words. Her letter shows a healthy fear—respect mixed with trust. She knew I was upset with her, but she also knew there were still tender feelings of commitment and love.

When she marries, she'll remember that friction doesn't need to lead to abuse, long-term distance, or fractured relationship. She has learned to trust and won't need to run from conflict.

A father's consistent discipline combined with a dad's devotion helps create a very wonderful thing: a trusting and mature young woman. I'd like to close this chapter with a letter from Holly. These thoughts were penned on a Father's Day card that she gave to me several years ago.

Dear Dad,

You really have given me a lifetime of wonderful memories. I still smile thinking about all the times we'd play Big Bad Wolf and you'd smoosh me in the cushions and then turn your back to get the mustard so I could escape . . . and I thought I was so smart!

And I still remember one night when you turned off all the lights and you walked down the hall with a flickering candle so we could see Huggy Hairy's shadow coming slowly towards our room . . . and I thought I was so brave.

And I remember all the times you held my hand through all those awful surgeries and you told me how brave I was to sit through an hour in a small MRI tunnel because you could never do it; and how you made our trip to Portland actually fun . . . and I thought I had been so alone.

And I remember a letter you wrote to me in college on three small Post-it notes, telling me how you remembered being twenty-one and thinking, "This is it?!" And being bewildered that you were an adult and yet you didn't feel like an adult. I still have those three faded Post-it notes on which you told me how you could relate and that you were proud of me . . . and I thought I was so independent.

And this last year, you have truly been my saving grace as you held me when I cried from a broken heart and listened to me for hours talk about my despair and frustration as I learned that even love at times has its limits. Your gentleness carried me through this year and your encouragement gave me the strength . . . and I thought I had been so right.

You have already given me more wonderful memories than I could ever write out. You make my life a thousand times brighter and I cannot tell you enough how much I love you. You truly are the best dad in the world and I don't know where I'd be without you. Thank you for all you have done and all you do for me . . . and I <u>know</u> how thankful I am for <u>you</u>!!

I love you, Dad!

Holly

This letter reveals a daughter's heart. We can't build trust with one grand gesture. We can't do it two weekends out of the month. Trust and relationship are built by having fun together, facing fears together, walking through sickness and injury together, and sharing heartache and pain. It is a lifetime journey with a wonderful destination.

Father—will you begin building trust in your daughter today?

CHAPTER 8
Blessing Kids with Failure

One of the most important things a father can do for a daughter is give her the freedom to fail.

Perfectionism devastates young women. The drive to always be right, always be pretty, and always be perfect has wreaked more havoc on the female half of the population than just about anything else I know.

The margin of error for today's young women is way too narrow. If they gain five pounds while growing, they think they're fat. If they get solid B's on their report card, they think they're dumb. If they don't get asked to go to a dance, they think they're ugly.

It's up to the father to accept his daughters, because young women need masculine approval that is freely given, not earned. A mother just is not able to give a daughter what she really needs—a male who delights in her, who adores her, who affirms her, and builds her up regardless of whether she's a klutz, wears a size-fourteen dress, or is just plain old average. A daughter should never feel "average" when she sees her reflection in her daddy's eyes.

I want my kids to know they can fail and that I'll love them just the same. My love isn't contingent on them being the prettiest, the most athletic, the smartest, and certainly not the thinnest.

Modeling Failure

As one who speaks a lot in the Christian community in the U.S. and Canada, I love to ask the congregation a sucker question: "Does anyone here tonight think they can be a better Christian?"

Almost without fail, virtually every hand will raise. Everyone thinks they need to do "better" as a Christian.

I love to deliver the knockout punch: "You know, the fact is, you *can't* be a better Christian. Wanting to become a 'better' Christian is a little bit like wanting to become 'better' pregnant. You're either pregnant or you're not; you're either a Christian or you're not. God doesn't give out letter grades, with some below-average Christians walking around with a D- on their report card, while a few superlative saints carry exams with an A+ written on the top. The way our faith is set up, it's pass/fail. You're in or you're out."

So many people tell themselves, "Someday my faith will be strong enough that I can be the kind of person God would have me to be." This is one of the unquestioned lies we tell ourselves, and it keeps us from really enjoying a relationship with almighty God.

I know what some of you are saying. "You don't understand my situation, Leman. I've got sin in my life. I'm working through some serious character problems."

That may be so, but my message will still be the same. God can use us, *imperfect as we are*, to help change this world.

As soon as I give this line in a seminar, I see heads nodding like star-lings on a fence post. Deep down, people know this, but we forget it, choosing instead to chase the elusive quality of perfection and unwit-tingly to limit ourselves and others around us, including our daughters.

I always like to chuckle when I think about "certain failures" who have succeeded beyond their wildest dreams, people like Zane Grey, one of the best-selling novelists of all time. At one point, publishers told him he couldn't write. Tell that to his hundreds of millions of read-ers. Many people thought Thomas Edison's elevator didn't go all the way to the top, and that Albert Einstein was a few fries short of a Happy Meal. A lot of brilliant people have been written off.

It's one thing when others write us off, but it's even worse when we write ourselves off. It breaks my heart to see young women doing this at an alarming rate. They never quite made it in their daddy's eyes. They looked in his face and saw judgment, disappointment, and criti-cism, and they internalized the thought that they have nothing to offer the world. They might have many fine qualities, but they know there's always someone who is just a little bit prettier, a bit more athletic, a half-grade smarter, and since they're not the best at anything, they think they're abject failures.

I'd like to break through this fog and shine a little light into dark households.

The Pharisaic Flash

Do you want to see a Pharisee's eyes flash? Then do what I love to do during my seminars.

"You know what Christian parents really need to do today?" I'll ask.

"Listen carefully, because this is one of the most important parenting lessons I've ever passed on. Are you ready? You need to flaunt your failures to your children."

I have to confess that talking like this is one of the most enjoyable things I do!

Too many Christians think they have to present this pristine, error-free image to their children: the "perfect Christian man," the "perfect Christian woman." In reality, this is one of the most damaging things you can do as a parent.

There's no getting around the fact that God calls me to be a model to my daughters, but the Bible is equally clear that I am an *imperfect* model. If daughters are going to learn how to handle their own failures in life, they need to see how their father has handled his failures—and that means he can't cover them up.

Lisa homeschools three children. One of her daughters was berating herself over an academic failure—she insisted she could never get it right, so what was the use trying?—when Lisa's husband, Greg, brought out a wad of papers. Greg is a full-time, professional musician, but he held in his hand one hundred fifty rejections that he had received over the eight years he spent trying to break into the music world.

"If I had given up that easily, Jessica," he said, "I wouldn't be doing what I love to do more than anything else in the world. Not getting something right on the first try doesn't mean you've failed—unless, that is, you quit. The best kind of success is often built on a foundation of multiple failures."

I honestly believe that one of the reasons my books have done so well and why I've been asked to appear on so many television shows is that I'm not your typical shrink. If you passed me on the street and didn't know who I was, there is no way you'd guess I was a professional psychologist. When I talk to teens, when I talk to parents, when I talk to anyone for that matter, I'm just a regular guy. I admit that I've learned as much from failure as I have from success. But far from turning people against me, this has the effect of helping them relate to me.

The same principle works in parenting. Be a regular guy with your kids. Let them know how you failed when you were their age and how you fail now so that they can learn from that failure.

And don't always see peace as bliss.

Problematic Peace

I recall that there was *one* day in the twenty-two years the older two girls lived together that there was *not* a squabble—and what a blessed day it was! Yet I don't see this as failed parenting. I don't think lack of conflict is necessarily a sign of maturity.

We live in a world of conflict, and it's essential that I teach my kids how to handle conflict. That's difficult to do if they never fight—sort of like trying to teach someone from the Congo to ski when they've never seen snow and have to pretend the sand under their feet is slippery.

This is part of blessing kids with failure. Most kids fight. The goal is not to stop all conflict, but to get them to learn how to resolve their conflict. Too many fathers are more concerned with peace and quiet than they are with character. A tyrant can enforce order, but who would want to live in Nazi Germany? Some things are more important than order.

Conflict extends beyond siblings to sometimes include fathers and daughters. Here, too, dads need to teach their girls how to overcome disagreements.

One morning, then three-year-old Lauren was teasing Barkley, our dog, as little girls are wont to do. (Barkley has an impeccable pedigree—we bought him from comedian Garry Shandling's mother.) Holding a dog biscuit in front of the dog, Lauren called out in her childish, singsong voice, "Barkley, want a treat, want a treat? Barkley, want a treat, want a treat?"

Krissy and I thought she looked so cute that we did the same thing to Lauren. "Lauren, want a treat, want a treat? Lauren, want a treat, want a treat?"

Without saying a word, Lauren slid off her stool and left the room.

"Uh-oh," Krissy said. "I don't think that went over very well."

I walked into the next room and watched as Lauren gave me "the look." She backed away from me as I drew near to her. Her bedroom was downstairs, and my youngest slowly worked her way to the top step. I moved forward one pace, so Lauren took one step back, down the stairs. I took another step forward; Lauren took another step back. Finally, she slid on her stomach all the way down the stairs and fled into her room, locking the door.

Krissy went down there to see if peace couldn't be made. "Lauren, honey," she said through the door, "we weren't making fun of you. We just thought you looked so cute and adorable, that's all."

With the tone that only an aggrieved child can muster, Lauren firmly announced, "You need to apologize."

"I'm really sorry, Lauren. Honest, I am."

"No, you need to write it down."

Keep in mind, Lauren was three years old. She couldn't even read yet, but Krissy dutifully obeyed. Even so, Lauren still wouldn't open the door.

"Daddy needs to apologize too," she said through the still-locked door.

I came downstairs and said my piece, but attorney Lauren repeated the same thing to me. "You need to write it down too."

I took out a piece of paper and wrote, "Lauren, I am very, very sorry. I love you. Daddy."

Only after two pieces of paper were slipped under the door was Lauren willing to open it up and resume relations.

I might have a difficult time telling the difference between a monkey wrench and a crescent wrench; I couldn't tell a carburetor from a starter; but one of the things I'm good at is saying, "I'm sorry." My family is not unfamiliar with those words.

I'm sorry is just about the most powerful recipe for intimacy between a father and a daughter I know. You can be the typical pontificating parent, smug in your foolishness, wounding your child without even knowing it, but as soon as you recognize your ridiculousness and say *I'm sorry*, that lion-hearted, defiant daughter will start purring like a kitten. She can't wait to forgive you.

Unless your parents' names are Mary and Joseph and you were born in a stable, you had better learn how to apologize. There has been only one perfect man on this planet, and buddy, you aren't Him! If it's particularly difficult for you to utter these words, practice saying the phrase the next time you're shaving. Start out with *I'm* and give yourself a ten-second pause. Then say *sorry*. The next time, cut the pause down to eight seconds, then six seconds, then four, then string the two words together. *I'm sorry*, spoken quickly, will be one of the most valuable tools you'll ever learn to use.

Apologizing as part of resolving conflict is just the first step in the art of modeling failure, however. You also need to let your daughters see how you handle life's most embarrassing moments.

You Won't Believe What I Did!

"So, kids, get this," I began. They love hearing stories about me meeting celebrities.

"This woman comes up to me and says, 'You are so right, you are exactly right, doctor!'

"'Who *is* this woman?' I asked myself.

"'Oh, by the way,' she said, 'I'm CeCe, Geraldo's wife.'"

I had just completed a segment on Geraldo Rivera's show, and CeCe wanted me to know how much she agreed with what I had to say.

I continued telling the story to my children. "Without even thinking of taking no for an answer, she led me into Geraldo's dressing room."

"Really, Daddy?" one of my daughters asked. "You were actually in his dressing room?"

"That's right," I said, "and then Geraldo came in and wanted to know what I was doing there with his wife!"

They all laughed.

"But her parents were there too. Still, Geraldo was thinking, *I thought we finished with this guy. Why's he hanging around?*"

"What happened next?" my kids wanted to know.

"Then I knocked Geraldo's beer onto the floor."

"*No!*"

"Yes, I did."

"Really?"

"I'm afraid so. It broke and spilled all over the place."

They laughed so hard I thought they'd need to make an emergency trip to the bathroom. "Really?" they squealed. "You knocked Geraldo's beer to the floor in his dressing room?"

"Darn right I did. It was a Heineken."

For some reason, they thought this was even funnier, and our family had a good laugh.

"I can't believe you knocked over Geraldo Rivera's beer," they kept saying.

What was going on, here? Middle school and high school—even grade school—kids often live in intense fear of being embarrassed. The worst thing that can happen to them, in many of their minds, is to be laughed at or to do something dumb. This is especially true of daughters. Their fragile psyches can be rocked for weeks over one careless remark uttered in a school cafeteria.

That's why I make it a practice to let my kids know about situations where I look really bad. Here I am, in a celebrity's dressing room, and what does suave Dr. Leman do? He knocks Rivera's beer onto the floor!

What this does is give my kids a more realistic view of life. Unfortunately, most kids view us only in an "ideal" atmosphere. They see us in the controlled home environment where we rule and rarely make a mistake. We're confident, self-assured, and in charge. That's fine, but how about letting them see us at work (I think take-your-daughter-to-work day is a great idea), where we might be a little less confident and even slightly in fear of our own boss? It might be humbling for you to have your daughters discover that someone else can order their daddy around. On the other hand, it will help them learn to be ordered around by their teacher—and you!

Sometimes taking my daughters to work means going to my counseling office here in Tucson. Other times it means taking my kids to meet Oprah or Phil Donahue or Regis and Kathie Lee. Even here, I am consciously trying to get my girls to gain a more realistic view of life. I want my daughters to know that these celebrities are real people. They look the way they do because they have someone who is paid top dollar to tease and coax their hair into a perfect arrangement. Someone else applies the makeup. Yet another person is in charge of acquiring personally tailored clothes.

Kids tend to amplify their own shortcomings and assume that others somehow walk on a cloud. Cindy Crawford wakes up with morning breath just like the rest of us; her hair has tangles too. Editors wouldn't dare put her picture on the cover of their magazines until she was worked over first.

By taking our daughters to work and recounting our own failures, we have a chance to remind our girls that there are going to be times when we will embarrass ourselves. That's part of life—it happens to everyone. Learning how to handle embarrassing situations is a necessary skill. I don't want them to respond to embarrassment by trying to embarrass somebody else. I want them to see how their dad handles it—and I want them to know that embarrassing things can happen to a man that they sometimes view as larger than life.

Teach your kids how *you* handle *your* embarrassments. Tell them your stories, and don't hold back on any of the self-incriminating details. It's great therapy for kids to be able to laugh along with their parents. It models for them that it's okay for us to laugh at ourselves. There's a security in this, and I believe it will help them develop a healthy sense of humor as well.

If you hold up an image of a man or woman who never fails, who is never laughed at, who never does anything embarrassing, your kids will feel all that much lower when they fail or do something embarrassing.

My kids know all about my foibles. They know I'm slightly claustrophobic. If you get on a flight on which I'm booked and you don't see me sitting in the front row seat, something is wrong. That's *my* seat. I have to sit there. I figure American Airlines can find three hundred other people who are perfectly willing to be boxed in; I fly enough that they can accommodate this one idiosyncrasy. Otherwise, I get this claustrophobic feeling that starts at the base of my spine and starts to tap-dance its way up my back.

What an inheritance it is to give our daughters the understanding, knowledge, and freedom that everyone has personal embarrassments, failures, and shortcomings. That knowledge will go a long way toward helping them develop the self-confidence they need to get through a cruel world. It will also help them avoid making disastrous long-term decisions.

In addition to teaching your daughter how to handle her failures and embarrassments, you'll need to help her cultivate a healthy and balanced view about success. I've noticed an increasing trend among well-meaning parents that has a dangerous underside. Let's talk a moment about our culture's addiction to achievement—and the pernicious influence it creates for a perfectionistic daughter.

Addicted to Achieving

When Holly first went away to college, our firstborn, straight-A student started pulling all C's. Years later, she was asked about this—specifically, how I reacted. This is how she responded:

"My dad didn't overreact. His attitude was more, 'They're your grades and it's your life; if these grades aren't good enough, you'll either bear the consequences or get the awards.'"

Throughout their schooling, I imprinted my daughters with the value of a good education. But I never led them to believe that grades were all that mattered. In fact, I sometimes went overboard in the other direction. When our kids got their report cards, they knew I paid more attention to the teacher's written character comments than I did to the actual grades. I wanted our children to know that what matters is the type of person you are, not the things you do.

We live in a society, however, that usually focuses on how much we can get done, and our children pay the price for our polluted perspective. A typical afternoon cell phone conversation goes like this:

"Bob, where are you?"

"I'm at the gym. Where's Ashley?"

"No! Monday night is karate! You're supposed to be at the rec center. Her teacher just called."

"I thought Monday nights were basketball."

"That's Tuesday, after Girl Scouts. You better get over to the rec center fast!"

"All right, I'm headed back to the car. By the way, what are we having for dinner?"

"I don't know. Megan's band practice is running late. Why don't you stop and get some burgers?"

If you tie a kid's self-esteem to achievement, you'll run the little buzzards ragged trying to find something they can excel in. That's why the Lemans aren't joiners. If you really want to help your kids, let them choose one extracurricular activity a semester.

The curse of suburbia is forcing kids to succeed *outside* the family.

With country folk, there's a much more healthy emphasis on giving back to the family. A child's sense of worth and belonging comes from contributing to the home life in which she has been nurtured and cared for. Her contribution might be as simple as milking a cow, feeding the chickens, or collecting eggs, but such a child grows up with a sense of belonging and purpose.

What can you do in the suburbs? Take out the garbage? Great—what will the kids do for the remaining twenty-three hours and fifty-five minutes of the day?

Somewhere around the 1960s, suburban parents found the "answer": Kids need to prove their worth outside the home. We have to find something they're the "best" in. If they fail at basketball, baseball, gymnastics, track, soccer, and chess, we try Girl Scouts, drama, piano lessons, art, spelling bees, you name it. And, whether we want it to or not, all this frenetic activity says one thing to our kids: Prove yourself.

I'm so glad I serve a God who says, "Kevin, I've proven *my* love for *you*," rather than "Prove yourself, Leman."

If you want to raise a well-adjusted daughter, don't run her into exhaustion in a vain effort at helping her finally prove herself. Prove *your* love. Prove *your* commitment. Prove *your* affection. That's what builds healthy kids.

CHAPTER 9
Love Them Differently

"She doesn't look like Holly."

It was eighteen months after our firstborn had reordered our lives when child number two, Krissy, made her grand entrance. I don't know what I expected. I guess part of me thought, *Same father, same mother, same kid, right? Or at least a reasonable facsimile.*

Not even close.

Holly entered this world with a long, narrow face. Krissy sported a Charlie Brown oval. Personality-wise, Holly is a stereotypical firstborn: as a kid she was bossy, tough as nails when she needed to be, and determined to run her younger siblings' lives. (She did that quite successfully for a number of years.) She was always trying to con Krissy. "Here, Krissy, see how much bigger this nickel is than your dime? Wanna trade?"

Krissy, living on the rebound, is extraordinarily relational, fun loving, and laid-back. When they were very young, you'd see eighteen-month-old Krissy wearing floaties in the pool, her little head bobbing back and forth, contentedly riding the waves without a care in the world. Holly would be networking with adults or organizing a performance.

It was inevitable, of course, that the two would become very competitive. Sometimes, the contests weren't all that fair. Holly regularly set up singing competitions, and she insisted that Sande and I serve as judges. The problem was, Krissy sang like a bird and Holly sang like . . . her mother. It wasn't even close.

I never understood why Holly kept insisting on these contests, as she simply did not have the equipment to knock off her younger sister. Finally, Sande and I grew tired of always giving first place to Krissy, so out of charity one time I finally said, "I think Holly won that one, don't you, honey?"

Krissy's face scrunched up into the funniest little ball of confusion you've ever seen. It's like she was saying, "What?! Did you hear what I heard?!"

Fortunately, Chuck Swindoll gave me a wonderful piece of advice. A lot of parents have misinterpreted Proverbs 22:6: "Train up a child in the way he should go, and when he is old he will not depart from it." They take that to mean that there is one prescribed way to raise a godly child and that our job as parents is to apply this one pattern to each son and daughter.

Chuck set me straight. "You know, Leman," he said, "that really translates as the 'individual bent' of each child. It doesn't mean train up a child in the way you *think* he should go."

As the author of *The New Birth Order Book*, let me tell you that I say "Amen!" to that. For men with multiple daughters, one of the most valuable slogans to learn is, "Love them differently." Become a student of your daughter, find out her individual bent, and raise her accordingly.

Too many parents get caught in the trap of even-steven. That's disastrous parenting, and it's impossible to achieve. Let me give an example here. Let's say you have two kids squabbling over a piece of cake. The even-steven parent—the very picture of naïveté—thinks he can solve this dilemma easily by getting out a knife. He slices the cake in two and with a big smile says, "Now you don't have to fight any more."

But his kids are smarter than he is.

"Her piece is bigger than mine," one says.

"Is not."

"Is too."

Even-steven parent, still wallowing in his innocence, comes up with brilliant plan number two. He gets out a ruler and measures the halves.

"See," he points out, "they're exactly the same size."

"Hers has more frosting," one daughter pouts.

Here's an end run. The next time you have two kids fighting over a piece of cake, hand one of them a knife and say, "You cut."

The other one may likely scream, "That's not fair! Why does she get to cut?" but proceed as planned.

After the cut has been made, turn to the other kid and say, "Okay, now you choose."

The next time these two face a similar situation, I guarantee you that the one doing the cutting will go out of her way to make the pieces as equal as possible.

Even-steven parenting has the opposite effect of what it intends: It makes natural competition all the more vicious. The truth is, kids want to feel special, not average. Each daughter is going to fight for her own share of Daddy's affection. They know they can't occupy the same place, so the discerning dad will help each daughter find her unique bond.

That's why it is so helpful for fathers as well as daughters to do their own family life maps, as we discussed in Chapter 3. If my male radar is correct, I bet some men skipped over this exercise. "Why do I need to do that?" Dad probably said to himself.

Life maps help a father learn how to use the family dynamics for good rather than ill. If the father clearly has an Eagle Scout firstborn, he can begin to devise some ways to make number two feel noticed without that child feeling that she has to break every rule just to get some attention.

It will also help a father critique his own feelings. Understand this: A father will tend to over-identify with the child who is in the same position as he is (firstborn, middle-born, or later-born). Likewise, you will probably butt heads more frequently with the child who has a personality that most closely resembles your own.

Without realizing it, if a father is a firstborn, he will naturally gravitate toward his firstborn child as surely as our planet spins around the sun. If he is the last-born, he will always have a special soft spot for the youngest. It's going to happen, so pay attention.

As I look back on my own parenting experience, I realize that I probably overprotected Krissy from Holly. Being the youngest born, I was sensitive to how older siblings can manipulate and rule. It was only natural that I should find myself becoming Krissy's protector. But realizing this has allowed me to compensate in my relationship with Holly—both of them think they're my favorite!

Let's look at how a father can love each child differently, as well as what he needs to watch out for with each segment in the birth order.

Troubling Tendencies

A friend of mine heard Holly talking about her now-famous singing contests with Krissy, and he asked her how it felt to be outshone by her younger sister. Holly's comments fascinated me, and confirmed my belief that we need to treat each child differently.

"The message my dad gave me was clear," Holly said. "Singing was my sister's gift, not mine. My talent lay in other areas, and I had to discover what those areas were." Holly didn't feel slighted that she rarely won the contest; she felt affirmed and directed toward her true strengths.

For the next several pages, we're going to look at what a father can expect of each daughter and how he can use that knowledge to love her differently. No, I've never met your daughters, but by nature of their birth order I can make some fairly accurate generalizations. As the dad, it'll be your job to customize that information so that you can raise each child according to her own particular bent.

Wearing All a Man's Dreams

As my firstborn, Holly has always struggled to maintain a certain measure of control. If you intruded on her plans, you paid the price. Early on, Sande and I debated over who woke Holly in the morning.

"Better get Holly up, honey," I'd say. "It's almost time to leave for preschool."

"*I'm* not waking her up," Sande insisted. "*You* wake her up. I woke her up yesterday."

Holly, as you might have guessed, woke up swinging. She was a tough kid, a four-year-old Judge Judy. And nobody was going to stand in her way.

At the age of four, Holly decided to drop out of preschool. She had had enough of the muddle-headed transformation that had gone on at that place of lower education. I've always said, "If you want to screw something up, hire a Ph.D." That's what they did when they turned

Holly's preschool from a warm, fuzzy experience into an experimental learning center. After the change, neither Holly nor I thought much of it, which is why I was prepared when she came home one afternoon and said, "I'm not going to preschool anymore."

"Well, Holly, if you're not going to preschool anymore, you have to call them and tell them."

"But I don't have their number."

Keep in mind, this is a four-year-old girl I'm talking about. I decided to call her bluff. "I'll get the number," I said.

Holly one-upped me. She dialed it. I don't know who answered, but she said, "This is Schlolly Leman" (she couldn't pronounce Holly). "I'm not coming to school there anymore."

She never went back.

When the firstborn pops out, many a dad is saying to himself, "This child is going to do everything I didn't do. This child will be everything I wasn't." Don't think for a minute that the child doesn't pick this up.

There's a healthy side to this—it is normal for fathers to desire good things for their children. But if fathers don't consciously recognize the temptation to project their unfulfilled dreams, particularly on their firstborns, they run the risk of strangling them and not raising them according to the child's God-given bent.

School is often the first proving ground in a firstborn's life. Expectations run high, and a little girl walking into kindergarten is wearing more than OshKosh overalls; she's wearing all her father's dreams.

New dads need to understand that what a first grader needs more than A's and B's is an accepting, loving, and affirming father. By the time the last-born gets through school, Dad's expectations won't be nearly so high. Just about every first-time father could loosen up in this regard.

School is *a* proving ground, not *the* proving ground. Remember—Bill Gates is a college dropout.

Firstborns also routinely get slammed for introducing their parents to the fact that a five-year-old can't control everything her body does quite as well as a thirty-five-year-old. When a firstborn child burps in public, the parent is likely to react as if the child had spewed a dozen profanities in the presence of their pastor.

"How could you do that? I'm so ashamed! Say, 'Excuse me,' right now. Don't ever let me catch you doing that in public again."

A little gas, and the poor kid gets four slams in four seconds.

Of course you want well-behaved and well-mannered children. We all do. But making the firstborn carry the honor of the family on her own five-, ten-, or even fifteen-year-old shoulders is asking too much. Try a simple, "Honey, you might want to cover your mouth when you burp. Thank you."

So, rule number one for your firstborn daughter: Lighten up! Firstborns already are burdened with a perceived need to be in charge and in control; they're *already* going to be serious, conservative, and good planners. The underside is that they are likely to be perfectionists, moody, stubborn, skeptical, tense, and critical. If you realize this ahead of time, you can steer them toward more tolerance, patience, and cooperation.

Mashed in the Middle

Hannah, our fourth born (of five), nearly worships her older brother, Kevin. As far as she's concerned, the sun's light comes from him. So I was quite taken aback when I heard her telling her brother, in no uncertain terms, that he was *not* coming with us to a movie that Hannah and I had made plans to attend. Kevin thought it might be fun to tag along, but Hannah was adamant: It would be just Daddy and her—no big brother!

Middle-borns crave time with their parents like babies crave milk. Theirs is a tenuous position, squeezed between the crown princess and little schnooky. Consequently, they always think they're getting the short end of the stick (and they usually are).

They look through the photo albums, and what do they find? The oldest has three full volumes chronicling the child's first two years. The albums are gold-gilded and bulging with Kodak moments. When she asks about her own photo albums, her parents hand her seven slightly crumpled pictures, five of which have the oldest putting her armpit around her.

"Why don't I have as many pictures?" she'll ask.

"We were *tired*, okay?" the parents say.

Middle-borns want time and attention because they often get less of it. The primacy of older children is firmly established, and the demands of the youngest child are often most urgent, so the needs of the middle-born get far less attention.

As the father of a middle-born, you need to be extra careful that you give as much of yourself as possible to your middle child(ren). If you don't willingly give them time, they'll often cause trouble just to get your attention.

Also, you need to be aware that the tendency of your middle-born will be to play off your oldest child. If the oldest is great in athletics, the middle may become a scholar, or vice versa. It is vital that you openly affirm the middle child without comparing him or her to the Miss America firstborn.

For example, something as simple as Middle-born Millie doing a handstand can create all kinds of conflict. Millie gets her feet up in the air and cries out, "Mom and Dad, look at me! I'm doing a handstand."

Without thinking, Dad turns to Mom and says, "Remember when Firstborn Felicia did that?"

What this dad just told Millie is that her older sister did two years ago what Millie only now did for the very first time.

I'll never catch up, she says to herself.

Don't let this happen. If you have five kids and have watched three of them learn to ride bikes, it's no less exciting to the fourth child when she learns—even though it's much less exciting to you. It's *her* first time and she still needs to see that acceptance and affirmation in her daddy's eyes.

One of the greatest challenges of fathering a middle-born daughter is overcoming the natural inferiority and neglect that plagues her birth order. She'll be less open with her feelings and much more peer dependent. You'll have to work hard at affirming her, and it will be difficult for you to draw her out. You'll need to pursue this daughter and convince her that you love her.

Little Princess

When our family travels, Lauren, as well as Sande and I, usually flies first class. We can't afford for the entire family to do this, so the older kids travel in coach. Since Lauren is still so young, we want her close by.

One time, just before we boarded a plane, Lauren looked up at her oldest sister and asked her, "Holly, how come whenever I get on the plane I never see you anymore?"

Big sis nearly exploded. "Because I'm buried back in twenty-four-D, that's why. You get to sit up front where there's oxygen and the guy in front of you isn't leaning back so far he's practically in your lap!"

By nature of needing to be protected a little bit more, the last-born is raised with a sense of entitlement. Besides, can anybody steal a father's heart like the last-born? Particularly if the last-born is a daughter?

For starters, it's almost certain that the youngest girl will have a pet name. The older kids will most likely be called by their given names; the youngest is just "too adorable," so she's given a cute nickname.

And don't think she doesn't notice—or that it passes the review of her older siblings.

This creates a situation in which the youngest tends to be the most manipulative, able to work Daddy into permissiveness just by batting her eyelids or letting a solitary tear slip out of a precious eye and stain that porcelain-perfect cheek. I've seen rock-hard negotiators, known in the business world for forcing grown men into humble compliance, who nevertheless melt before the disparaging look of their three-year-old youngest daughter.

"So what's the danger?" you might ask. The risk is this: If you let little schnooky get away with this behavior, she'll marry someone just like you—somebody she can manipulate and control.

Though last-borns generally have the positive qualities of being tolerant, easygoing, caring, and empathetic, you'll also find your youngest daughter irritating you by being impulsive, irresponsible, disorganized, and self-centered.

Now that you know the tendency of each child in the birth order, take a few moments to consider your own family. How can you make the middle-born feel accepted? How can you help the last-born learn to be less selfish? How can you get the firstborn to lighten up? Become proactive here, making a plan to love your kids differently. Maybe you could plan a special date between you and daughter number two.

Perhaps you need to apologize to daughter number one, or to get tougher with daughter number three.

Whatever you decide, remember that it is important to love them differently. That means finding unique ways to make each one feel special.

Making Kids Feel Special

"Daddy, I really want a keyboard for Christmas," Krissy pronounced late one fall. For the next several weeks, she wouldn't let me or Sande forget it. We received an updated bulletin on her increasing desire two or three times a day. As an exclamation point, Krissy pretended to play a keyboard during breakfast and dinner. She talked about where she would put it. She made it clear that if only she had a keyboard she would be the happiest girl in the universe.

On Christmas morning, Krissy's dreams were realized. Unwittingly, we unlocked the nightmares of another.

I had completely forgotten that Holly had been the first one to ask for a keyboard. In typical fashion for her, however, Holly mentioned it just once, then forgot about it. Krissy jumped on the bandwagon and never let it go. It had become a competition, and we didn't even know it.

After all the presents were unwrapped, Holly was furious. We had the quietest week after Christmas I have ever known—before or since. Holly's fury was such that she brought winter's chill inside. People were afraid to speak lest somehow Holly would transform it into another picture of the slight she had received at Christmas. Giving Krissy—and not Holly—the keyboard was like waving a red flag in front of a bull.

Most families have stories like this. So many parents run themselves ragged in December, and then spend a panicked Christmas Eve counting up the presents and realizing that one child obviously has more than the other.

One solution to this is to cut back on everybody. The other is to shun the notion that all kids should be treated alike. Some years, a child may need a bigger gift—a bicycle or a play house, for instance—which may restrict the parents' capacity to spend as much on the other children.

That's okay. It's actually healthy for kids at times to feel singled out. Other times, they may feel slighted, but as long as there are times when they feel honored, they'll come out ahead.

I've already mentioned that I'm not a big gift giver when I come home from a trip, wanting the focus to be on the renewal of relationship rather than on some trinkets in Daddy's suitcase. I do make occasional exceptions, however, particularly if I see something that fits one of my children unusually well.

One of my favorite stops over the years has been on the *700 Club*. I've appeared on that show twenty times or more. In the early days, before the Founders Inn was built, guests stayed in a hotel that was next to a very good mini-mall. One of the stores in that mall carried a cute little lamp, easily small enough to carry back on the plane. As soon as I saw it, I knew it would be a perfect gift for Krissy. She had been needing one for quite some time, and it was just her style.

I bought it.

When I walked in the door, Nancy Drew, expertly masquerading as my oldest daughter, Holly, greeted me. "What's in the box?" Holly asked.

"Oh, that's for Krissy."

"What do you mean that's for Krissy?"

"It means it's for Krissy. What other interpretation could you possibly come up with?"

144

Holly hung on me like a pit bull. "You brought home a gift? For Krissy?"

"What, you expect me to sell this to her for a profit?"

"Well, what did you bring me?" Her tone was defiant.

"Nothing."

"That's not fair!" Holly protested, collapsing into tears.

I held Holly and waited for the tears to subside before I asked her, "Holly, do you really want me to treat you the way I treat your little sister?"

"Yes." *Sniffle, sniffle.*

"Okay, your bedtime is now eight-thirty instead of nine."

The sniffles suddenly stopped.

"Oh, and your allowance is now two dollars instead of three dollars."

"What?!!"

"You said you wanted to be treated the same."

"I didn't mean *that*."

The point was made. "I *do* treat you differently," I said. "Because you are different. As the oldest, your allowance is bigger. You have more freedom, and a bit more responsibility. You of all the kids should be able to understand that from time to time I may find something that is perfect for one of you. But that doesn't obligate me to try to come up with a meaningless gift for everyone else, all in the name of some elusive thing called fairness."

It is impossible, from your kids' perspective, to treat them exactly the same. Even if you spent the same amount, down to the last penny, on Christmas gifts, one of the children would feel slighted, because the gift-giving wouldn't *feel* the same.

The reality is, every kid wants his or her day in the sun. Favor *all* your kids from time to time. Lauren knows she has an extra special place in Dad's heart because she's his youngest born. Holly knows she holds a unique place in my affection that no other child will ever have because she is the firstborn. I once wondered if I could ever love another child as much as I loved her (until Krissy and the others came along and I discovered that love isn't limited by numbers).

Every child has her own place with me. For years I spent Saturday mornings reading the newspaper with Holly. Krissy had no interest in what was happening, frankly, and Kevin II was always off doing something else, so Holly and I made a tradition of reading the paper together and talking over the news. We fell into a routine—I immediately handed her the "Life" and "Dear Abby" sections, and she knew I got to read the sports section first.

Because of this, I spent far more time talking about world and national events with Holly than I ever did with any of the other kids, but that's okay. That was part of our special relationship.

I tried to apply this even in the smallest decisions. On Fridays, I always brought the kids a treat from a bakery. I suppose it would have been easiest to simply tell the baker, "Give me half a dozen maple bars," but that wouldn't have been nearly as meaningful to my children. Instead, I picked out what I knew they liked best.

Holly and Kevin both wanted chocolate éclairs, all the time. Hannah liked a little more variety. Sometimes I'd get her an éclair and sometimes I'd get her a doughnut. Lauren had to have a doughnut *with sprinkles*. She liked to lick off the sprinkles and frosting and then throw away the rest. Since she never ate the cake part, she wouldn't know what to do with an éclair. Krissy liked these dainty little cakes called *petits fours*.

Every Friday, with this simple act, I reinforced the following message to my children: "There are five of you, but I know each one of you very well. I don't take you for granted. I never forget that you are individuals. You matter to me."

I want all my kids to feel special. That's one of the best gifts a father can give his daughter. Part of making a daughter feel special is letting her know that you know her well—and that you use that knowledge to raise her. On one occasion, I had to use this understanding to make one of the most difficult decisions I've ever made as a father.

Two Weeks

Much to her father's consternation, Krissy applied to just *one* college: North Park University in Chicago. It shouldn't have surprised me that a middle-born would place all her eggs in one basket, but even realizing this didn't make me feel all that comfortable with it.

Krissy was attracted to North Park for a variety of reasons. She had a lot of friends there, and the school administration, decades before, had had the good sense to kick out her father (though years later, they actually gave me the distinguished alumnus award!).

I knew the campus well, but I looked at it a bit differently now that I realized it would house my daughter. Move-in day was packed; we did all the things you do when you take a kid to college—meet the staff, haul suitcases to the dorm room, get acquainted with the roommate.

That night there was an orientation dinner. A long line formed for the students and their parents to personally meet the president of the university.

As Sande, Krissy, and I inched our way near the front, we were perhaps seven places away from shaking the president's hand when Krissy turned to me and said, "I need to talk to you."

"What do you mean, you need to talk to me? The president is right there. We've been waiting in line . . ."

"I need to talk to you right *now*."

"All right, come over here."

We stepped out of line, but Sande held our place. Any hope that this would be a short conversation was immediately dispelled when I saw the tears well up in Krissy's eyes.

"I don't want to go to school here."

"What?"

Keep in mind, this was the *only* school Krissy had applied to, and it was late August. She had no other options. Even so, she insisted, "I don't want to go to school here."

"Krissy," I said, "just get back in line."

"Daddy, I'm scared. I don't feel safe here. Please, don't make me stay here. I want to go home with you and Mom."

Earlier in the day, some creepy yahoo driving a truck had scared Krissy half to death when he raced through an alley at about forty miles an hour. Krissy was in that alley and just barely dodged the vehicle.

Few words get a father's attention more than *I don't feel safe here*. But I knew this wasn't the time to make a snap decision.

"Listen," I said, "we're going to shake the president's hand. See your mother? She's almost at the front. And then we're going to sit down and enjoy this chicken dinner together as a family. We'll talk more after that."

Crestfallen, Krissy slipped back in line. Needless to say, it was a very long dinner. Krissy didn't eat a thing. She didn't even try to make an effort to talk to the kids who were seated across from her.

We got through the dinner, went back to her dorm, and immediately noticed that when Sande and I had been attending parent functions, thinking Krissy was unpacking, daughter number two hadn't unpacked a single item. Not even a sock.

This was going to be tougher than I thought. Fortunately, God sent a kid to us. An upperclassman who had known Krissy from summer camp stopped by to see how she was doing. He sat and talked with her about how nervous and scared he was when he first came to college.

Unfortunately, after he left, Krissy was still determined to go home. "I don't feel safe here," she repeated, and that's when I had to do one of the toughest things I have ever done as a dad: I left her there anyway.

"Honey," I told her, "I know you're unhappy and upset with us and you want to come home, but I'm not going to take you out of here. This is a new situation, and you've never been one to love new situations. I believe in you and my guess is this college is going to work out, but here's my guarantee: If you still feel the same way in two weeks, I will personally fly out and bring you home."

Krissy had to leave for one last, but brief, meeting. While she was gone, I quickly wrote her a note that she could read when I was gone. I told her how proud I was of her, how confident I was that she was going to be okay. Later, she told me that when she read that letter, she "cried her eyes out." She needed me to be firm, but she also needed me to be tender; the letter accomplished both.

Sande and I faced another silent trip after dropping a daughter off at college. This was getting old.

We received several calls and letters from Krissy over the next fourteen days. Two weeks to the day after we dropped her off, I called her on the phone and said, "Well, Krissy, your two weeks are up."

"What two weeks?"

"Krissy," I said, incredulous, "the *two weeks*. Do you want me to fly out there and bring you home?"

"Dad," Krissy answered, sounding every bit like the teenager she was, "get real." She went on to tell me how wonderful school was. Her freshman class had gone to downtown Chicago (the Loop), she was meeting new friends, enjoying her classes . . .

For once, the psychologist and his lovely bride played it right. We rolled the dice and came up with sevens. We had based our decision on knowing Krissy's personal makeup, her individual bent. We didn't treat Krissy like we treated Holly; nor did we treat her like I would have handled Kevin II. We treated Krissy like Krissy.

The Power of Distinct Love

Knowing Krissy, I realized it wouldn't be fair to abandon her at North Park, even though she had begun to settle in. It was only a matter of time, I was sure, until she once again started feeling homesick. I thus made it a regular practice to arrange for long layovers in Chicago. The airlines will allow you to stay at an airport for up to four hours before you catch the next plane without charging you for that airport being a separate destination.

The first time I did this, I wanted it to be special, so I arrived at the school without giving Krissy advance notice. I had to go to Old Main to find out where Krissy would be, and I made sure to give myself enough time to get there before she did. I learned she was scheduled to be in a cell biology class, which met in an auditorium.

Ten minutes later, she was walking toward class when she saw her old man hanging out front. Her jaw dropped open, her face lit up, and the love that illuminated her face made me so glad I had taken the time to do this.

"How'd you know where I'd be?" she cried out.

"I went to Old Main and asked them."

"That is so cool," she said, incredulous.

She felt special. For those two-and a-half hours, she knew she was in the center of her father's heart. We had a great time eating lunch, talking, catching up on each other's lives.

This continued throughout Krissy's stay in college. During Krissy's sophomore year, Sande and I vacationed in Mexico. We knew from Krissy's letters that she was facing another down time, so on the return trip home I convinced the airline to give us a ticket that would take us from Mexico City to Arizona via the convenient route of Chicago! You have to have a bevy of frequent flyer miles to get that favor, but once it was done, we eagerly anticipated the surprise.

Knowing how young women hate to be embarrassed, especially by their parents, Sande and I showed up at Krissy's dorm wearing sombreros and Mexican blankets. We fit into the Chicago, academic yuppie scene about as well as a ham dinner at a synagogue. Wanting to really spring the surprise, we simply passed on the following message: "Tell Krissy Leman she has a package waiting for her downstairs."

When Krissy came down to get her package, there were the *two* amigos!

With each daughter, we have worked hard to study her character and apply a distinct style of parenting that fits her personality. While there has always been a great deal of competition between our two oldest daughters, rejecting the failed methods of even-steven parenting and instead trying to make each daughter feel special has paid big dividends.

Like so many aspects of parenting, this power of "distinct love" may reveal itself only in the long term. Sande and I received tremendous affirmation on the day Krissy was married. In a letter written to her sister, Krissy told Holly—her maid of honor—how she was a little nervous about getting married first. "You've always gone first," she reminded her big sis. "And I never have liked going first. That's probably why God gave me such a special sister like you. It can't be easy being at the top, knowing your four siblings are all looking up to you."

In that letter, Krissy acknowledged Holly's special role as the firstborn, but you can see for yourself that these words were penned without any malice; rather, they were couched in affection and affirmation.

"I want you to know how very special you are to me and how I treasure all the memories," Krissy's letter continued. "I love you with all of my heart. Thank you for standing next to me as I marry Den. It means so much to me that you're there.

"Thanks for being so special. I pray we will always remain close in heart, even though we'll be living in different states. I love you! Kris."

As a father, holding this letter in my hand was one of those rare moments, an absolutely delightful awareness that the wet cement has hardened and the result is a very pleasant surprise—siblings who love one another into adulthood.

"Krissy will do okay," I told myself. "She'll make it."

I've found few things so rewarding as making each of my daughters feel special, knowing each one's quirks, fears, dreams, hopes, and then parenting around those. Once again, we can learn a lesson from the greatest of all movies, *The Three Amigos*. Notorious bandit El Guapo tells his men, "I know each of you like I know my own smell."

As a parent, we should know our kids no less than El Guapo knows his men. The challenge is this: Can you make each kid feel special in her own way? We should know our children's scents and sense; their fears and tears; their dreams and their screams. Only then can we make the decision that is right for each daughter. If we take the time to get to know them this well, loving them differently will be a natural response.

CHAPTER 10

God Doesn't Want to Be First in Your Daughter's Life

A woman who used to work for me now lives in Kansas. She's elderly and retired, and I pestered her for years, so she deserves a rest. Even so, I can't help myself. I still like have to have fun with her.

One evening I called her up and when she answered the phone, I announced, "This is an obscene phone call!"

"Oh," this sweet woman politely responded, oblivious to who was on the other line. "I'm not interested."

Once she found out it was me, she was delighted to talk.

Now, try to remember the way we often introduce our children to God. "That's right, Jason. You have to take a bath. God doesn't like it when boys are dirty behind the ears."

"Of course you have to wear uncomfortable shoes, Missy. You're going to God's house. You think He wants you wearing sneakers?"

"No, you can't chew gum! We're supposed to worship. Remember, no talking, either, and certainly no snickering. This is a place of prayer and reverence."

You show me one five-year-old child who is going to look forward to visiting anybody's house that holds these rules. If we don't talk about God at home, however, this is the only introduction that a child will have: God doesn't like me to have any fun, He wants me to wear uncomfortable clothes, and He isn't interested in any of the things that normally interest me.

What saddens me about this is that I believe the presence of God is the most rewarding thing you can give to a daughter. I'm not talking about church, here (though of course I believe regular attendance in a house of worship is essential). I'm talking about a real relationship in which a child grows up knowing she is loved and watched over by her Father in heaven. If a child has this knowledge, she's going to be sought out, as my son was.

Kevin II attends a specialized art school in Florida. He was walking across campus one day when a young woman came up and stopped him.

"Can I ask you something?" she asked.

"Sure," Kevin said.

"Why are you always so happy?"

"You really want to know?"

"Yeah, that's why I'm asking."

"Well, I come from a really neat family, and I love God."

If we can give kids those two things—a "really neat family" and a love for God—everything else will fall into place for them. They'll make wise choices. They'll hang around the right people. They'll become the people God created them to be, and others will ask them, "How can I get what you have?"

But please don't turn this love for God into a boring obligation. When people talk about having devotions, my radar goes up. It's not that I think there is something wrong with devotions; it's just that I think we often use the word in the wrong way.

Instead of seeing *devotion* as a set time, I like to ask parents, "Do you practice devotion to your family every day? Do your kids see your devotion to God? Do your daughters see you hand the clerk at the grocery store her money back when she makes a mistake and gives you too much change? Do they see devotion as a daily element in your life?"

The best way to build faith in a child is to be an involved father who loves the Lord. Like it or not, men, in the early years your daughters will directly connect you with God. I've heard stories where young toddlers ended up "praying" to Daddy. That's why it is so crucial that you be an interested and active father especially during these years. When your daughter sees how you get involved in her day-to-day activities, she'll learn that her heavenly Father is equally concerned about all areas of her life.

In other words, instead of being obsessed about teaching her to pray a rote prayer, prove to her that you care. Then praying will come naturally.

In his book *Butterfly Kisses*, Bob Carlisle shares a touching tribute written by a daughter named Kelly Graham, to her father, Jack Graham:

Dear Daddy,

Words can never truly express how much I love, appreciate, and admire you. Through the years you have taught me so many important lessons. When I was little you showed me how to ride a bicycle and taught me patience. When we moved and I was having a hard time adjusting, you taught me how to stick out the tough times. When I was having trouble with my math grades, you encouraged me to do my best. When I had to come home from college with mono, you showed me compassion. Your relationship with Mom has taught me faithfulness and how to have a successful marriage.

All those lessons were important, but teaching me about priorities was perhaps the most important. You always taught me Jesus first, others second, yourself last. You have taught me this mainly by being an incredible example. I love you so much, and I could never repay how much you have given me. I am truly proud to call you my dad.[1]

Notice what Kelly wrote. Because her dad took the time to teach her how to ride a bike, get through math, and survive mono, she learned she could trust him when he also said that loving Jesus was the most important thing she could ever do. It's my contention that when Jack took the time to teach Kelly how to pedal wheels and divide fractions, he was setting her up for a great walk with God, every bit as much as when he talked specifically about devotions.

Devout Devotion

"Honey, Daddy has to go away on a trip tomorrow," I told my daughter.
"Ooooooohhh."
"Honey, remember, what are you going to do?"
"I'm gonna pray for you."
"And what am I gonna do?"
"You're gonna pray special just for me."
"That's right, and I'll be back in just two dark naps."
What's going on here? I'm trying to apply Deuteronomy 6:6–7 (NKJV):

And these words which I command you today shall be in your heart. You shall teach them diligently to your children, and shall talk of them when you sit in your house, when you walk by the way, when you lie down, and when you rise up.

You won't find me sitting my children down and going over some boring book to have devotions. That's because I believe daughters need to see daddies who don't place God number one in their lives; they need to see daddies who have God fill every area of their lives.

God is not interested in CNN-type polls, watching to see whether He narrowly ekes out a popular stand over whatever is number two in your life. God wants to be in everything we do. In the workplace, with our spouses, with our kids—you don't give God a number. He's above that. He wants your entire life, not just a majority of your life.

This is important because our daughters will look up to their daddies to make sense of this being we call God. Many young daughters shape their view of God largely by how they view their father. Even as they mature and begin to see more of their father's faults and certainly no longer think of him as all-powerful and all-knowing (in fact, they may think he's grown rather dumb), they're going to pick up about how this man relates to the Creator of the universe.

That's why I urge you not to give God a number but to give Him yourself. Don't segregate God; open up the whole house. Let prayer be a normal response to life, not an artificial stimulant that you inject into the family life in times of tragedy or stress.

My good friend Gary Smalley got an urgent call one night. His daughter, Kari, was pregnant with her second child. She was just nineteen weeks along when she began lapsing into premature labor. It was so serious, she had to spend over two months in the intensive care unit.

When she called Gary, she told her dad she felt miserable and that she had lost her appetite.

"Will you pray for me, Dad?" she asked.

"Sure, honey," Smalley said. He asked God to do two things: Let Kari wake up feeling happy and hungry.

God answered that prayer. Kari consumed no less than five bowls of cereal the next morning, but this full breakfast elicited another call a few days later. "Dad," Kari said, "I want you to keep praying for me, but only to be happy, not hungry. I've gained five pounds!"

What a wonderful picture: a father and daughter continue having a close relationship into adulthood, in which God remains in the middle.

And God doesn't need a prayer room to communicate with our daughters.

The Problematic Prayer Room

"Daddy, can I pray when I'm sitting on the toilet?"

Boy, I didn't remember reading anything about this in the Bible! "Sure, honey," I finally said. "You can pray anywhere."

While I respect what families and churches are trying to do when they construct prayer rooms, I think there is also a great danger in that approach. I don't want my kids to think that prayer is reserved for holy rooms. I want them to know that they can pray in their bedrooms, in the living room, outside in the field, in a car, and, yes, even in the bathroom.

As a kid I prayed at home plate a lot. Especially if Norm Hankinson of the Little League White Sox was on the mound. He was one of those eleven-year-olds who needed to shave. Preadolescent testosterone dripped off him as he sweat out on that mound, and his fastballs were terrifying to behold.

Apparently, the prayers worked. Even facing down Norm's fastballs, I was chosen to be on the all-star team.

A couple of decades later, I was trying to teach Kevin II how to play baseball, and on one occasion, he confessed that sometimes he got a bit nervous walking up to the plate.

"What did you do when you had to face Norm Hankinson?" Kevin asked me.

"Listen, Kevin. The plate is where I learned to pray."

The next time I saw Kevin II approaching the plate, I couldn't help but notice how he paused, scrunched his eyes closed for a few brief seconds, then took his place in the batter's box.

He was praying.

That's what devotion is all about. God cares about baseball—if a nine-year-old boy who loves Him is nervous about it.

Your daughter needs to see how prayer is relevant to her life, and the best way she can learn that is by seeing how prayer is relevant to her father's life.

A daddy does even more than make prayer seem relevant. By virtue of our position, we also represent authority to our daughters. How we model and handle that authority will greatly influence how our daughters learn to submit to God's authority.

Authority

Media mogul Ted Turner jumped tracks. He was a firstborn, but he has ended up acting like a middle-born maverick, completely changing the way television is done. What happened?

Frank Sulloway, a researcher at MIT, explained the process to *Forbes* magazine: "[Ted Turner] is the perfect example of a firstborn who had a lot of conflict with his parents. If firstborns don't identify with their parents, they'll behave like later-borns, especially in their rejection of conventional authority."[2]

Sulloway noted that Turner was severely disciplined and frequently abused by his dad. He was sent away to a military school when he was very young, thus facing rejection and distance, until his father later committed suicide. Ted has been thumbing his nose at the business establishment ever since (quite successfully, by the way).

What is true for men works for women as well—a father's ability or inability to handle authority will greatly affect his child's ability to come to grips with the establishment—including God.

One of the best ways for a father to turn his daughter on to God is to be a man who knows how to handle authority. It is an awesome, inescapable responsibility: Fathers model God to their children. Your son or daughter will be much less likely to accept the absolute authority of God the Father if they are unable to accept the authority of their father in the home.

This is one of the most perilous aspects of growing up fatherless. In such households, there is likely to be a spiritual ache that pervades a young woman's soul. When you see a woman really struggling in her faith—particularly if you talk to her and discover that her view of God is largely a big guy in the sky with a Wham-O slingshot ready to knock her off—odds are, you're looking at a woman who lacked a strong father figure when she was growing up.

That's why some Christians feel they have to get "saved" every weekend. They have no sense of divine acceptance, in large part because they were never intimate with their father. They never rested in the accepting arms of their daddy. So they can't imagine how the Creator God—the Divine Daddy—could accept them.

I remember when we built our second home. Before it was finished, I walked downstairs to check out everything and noticed a crack in one of the wood planks on the steps. I brought it to the contractor's attention, and he assured me it would be taken care of.

It wasn't. To this day, when you walk down those stairs you can feel a certain leeway in that one step. It looks beautiful on the outside, but underneath, a tiny crack has made that step unstable.

A missing father is more than a tiny crack. The gap left by a missing father can feel like a spiritual black hole that sucks up everything you try to pour into it. Spirituality is built from the ground up, beginning with the father's presence and the father's comfortableness with handling and using authority.

If you're concerned about whether you're measuring up as a dad in this regard, I encourage you to go back and reread Chapter 5, "A Good Dad." If you build the kind of relationship with your daughter described in that chapter, your daughter will have little problem accepting God's authority.

Dad, you can't take shortcuts here. Your parenting in this area will have eternal results—for good or for ill. You can help pass on the very meaning of life.

The Meaning of Life

Lauren made her radio debut when she was just a baby. Sande and our newest child came into the studio for a *Parent Talk* program, and Sande shared our initial struggle coming to grips with Lauren's conception, followed by a recounting of how joyful and thankful we had become for this "little gift from God."

I sent the older kids a tape of the program, and Krissy sent a letter to Sande in response. In the note, Krissy touched on a theme that I believe is profound.

"On the program today you talked about having two miscarriages before you had Holly. A thought popped into my mind after hearing that. I guess I've always thought that miscarried babies, and babies that were aborted, would go straight to heaven. If that thinking is right, then both Grandpa Leman and Grandma Buchheit have seen two of the children we haven't seen. That brings a tremendous amount of joy to me.

"I hope Grandma B. told Grandpa all about Hannah, and your expecting Lauren. I hope that is possible." (Krissy's paternal grandfather died before her maternal grandmother, so she was hoping that the one who died later could update the former on the family news!)

Faith ties a family together across generations. The truth of heaven is the glue that holds mother and father, son and daughter, grandson and granddaughter, and great grandson and great granddaughter in a complete circle of love. Heaven is the one thing that makes this crazy world make sense. Even when a precious family member dies, faith means we have hope that eventually we will be reunited.

Notice that Krissy said the thought of miscarried children being reunited with her deceased grandparents "brings a tremendous amount of joy to me." Faith gives kids an extra inheritance of belonging. They realize their family extends beyond this earth to include God's family. Belief in God's kingdom provides just one more element of stability, security, acceptance, and affirmation.

Belief will also prepare our daughters for old age, when we can't be there.

When Papa Passes

She was a precious woman—eighty-five, at least, perhaps closer to ninety—and she moved with a frailty that made her bones seem positively chalk-like. She was depressed and unsure she wanted to keep living.

"Everybody else is gone," she explained in a tired, soft voice. As the youngest in her family, both her parents and all her siblings had preceded her into eternity. Many of her friends were gone. Those who still remained were often prevented by their physical condition from traveling for a visit.

She felt terribly alone.

You know what hit me as I looked at that woman?

That's Lauren.

Her oldest sister is over twenty years ahead of her. Her parents will depart this world, in all likelihood, before Lauren is forty years old. Though Lauren is such a young, happy child today, it would break my heart to see her as a lonely, aging woman eight decades hence.

And yet it's possible. That's the inevitable cycle of life.

As much as I treasure being Lauren's father, I realize I can't be present in her life (physically, at least) forever. That would tear me up inside, except for the fact that I know Lauren has what she needs even more than a living earthly father—a heavenly Father.

Dads, we won't be there in our daughter's old age. That's why it is so vital that we turn them on to their heavenly Father. I don't want to offend anyone with this comment—please understand my heart here— but it's true that very elderly women (and men, for that matter) often begin to act more like children than adults. They once again become physically dependent. They need to be reminded to take their medicine. They may not be able to live alone.

When Lauren reaches that age, she'll need a father once again—and I won't be there. But God will, if she learns to recognize Him in her youth. This may not completely take away the loneliness that is so common among the elderly, but at the very least it will take away some of the sting.

This is so crucial—a good father learns to transfer his daughter's allegiance from himself to two others: her God and her husband. We must work our way out of our jobs for the simple reason that someday we will not be present to fulfill a father's duties. Our girls must learn to depend on someone else. Dads, there is no better inheritance you can give your daughter than the inheritance of faith.

Forget about making God number one.

Make God everything.

CHAPTER 11
Teach Your Daughter
That Other People Matter More

I got a call from Chuck Colson's prison ministry asking me to break one of my cardinal rules. Normally, I don't emcee. Okay, better tell the truth here. I *never* emcee. I'm happy to speak at a dinner, but I don't like to moderate. That's just not my style.

But I believe so strongly in what Colson's ministry does that I gave my consent. "It's the Monday after Easter," I was told, and my calendar was clear.

"Count me in," I said hurriedly—and repented greatly at leisure.

As fate would have it, my alma mater, the University of Arizona—of which I'm a big Cat fan, by the way, always sitting six rows up from the court—proceeded to charge through March Madness and play their way into the men's NCAA Final Four collegiate basketball tournament. As a big Cat, I got big seats—sixteen rows up—for one of the most coveted events in all of sports. You just cannot get these seats unless you know somebody.

I was elated at my alma mater's success until I realized that the final game of the Final Four tournament would be played the Monday after Easter.

167

I just about died. In fact, I spent a furious forty-eight hours trying to figure out a legitimate excuse to bag the benefit dinner and take my rightful place sixteen rows up to watch the Wildcats mount their assault on the national title. After all, the last time Arizona had played for the national championship was *never.* Who knows when it will happen again?

But it was no use. I had given my word. And the ministry was worth sacrificing for. Even, dare I say it, if that meant sacrificing great seats to the Final Four.

Our daughters grow up with messages that exalt love of self. "Learning to love yourself," the successful pop singer Whitney Houston belts out, "is the greatest love of all."

While I have no problem with cultivating a healthy dose of self-confidence and self-esteem, the danger of this message is that young women will put themselves first above everything else. But Jesus' words—we find our life by losing it—is as true for a fourteen-year-old girl as it is for a grown man or woman.

Other-centeredness is, ironically, crucial for our daughter's happiness. A young woman who lives only to be noticed will always be frustrated, because she will never be noticed enough. Even if she becomes a supermodel, her career will be limited to five or ten years (if that) until age takes its toll and makes her looks "unsuitable" for the editors of *Vogue* and *Glamour.* She will become bitter at the loss of what she valued most—fleeting beauty and youth.

On the other hand, a young woman who seeks to notice others will always be fulfilled, because there is an endless supply of people who need to be noticed and appreciated. She will find that meaning and contentment grow as she ages.

Our daughters need to see their fathers placing duty above happiness—or placing emceeing above the Final Four, as the case may be—so that they, too, can learn to be lost in a cause or purpose greater than themselves. I'd like to think they might be inclined to sacrificial service.

Sacrificial Service

Kathleen Kennedy Townsend knows how to get something done. On one occasion, she met a reporter from *Good Housekeeping* at a restaurant that didn't have milkshakes on the menu. Kathleen reasoned that a restaurant that serves both milk and chocolate ice cream should be able to create a chocolate milkshake, if asked.

The waiter, of course, assured Robert F. Kennedy's daughter that the restaurant didn't serve milkshakes, so Kathleen left the reporter behind and pushed past the waiter, disappearing into the kitchen. Several minutes later, she returned with a milkshake in hand.

Kathleen has spent most of her adult life in public service. Her father was assassinated when she was just seventeen years old, but that hasn't kept her from running for office. Following an unsuccessful bid for Congress, she sought and won a seat as Maryland's first female lieutenant governor.

As her state's second-ranking politician, Townsend developed the first statewide initiative in the nation that systematically targets crime hotspots by pulling together previously scattered government agency operations—community policing, probation enforcement, nuisance abatement, youth violence prevention, and community mobilization.

According to Kathleen, one of the things that helped prepare her to get things done is that "my father believed in setting difficult courses for children because that made them stretch to become more. My father's credo was: Try . . . Don't give up . . . Win!"

When you listen to Kathleen describe her father, you realize that Robert Kennedy did many things right. His daughter said that from him she learned "tough-minded men can be kind and sensitive. He was a very loving father."[1]

Robert Kennedy may have been sensitive and involved, yet he taught his daughter the hard-minded truths of trying, refusing to give up, and, ultimately, winning. He did more in the seventeen years he had with Kathleen than many fathers do over six or seven decades.

Have you taught your daughter the importance of serving? Does she know that life becomes more fulfilling when she concerns herself with making a difference in her community rather than spending three hours a day in the gym trying to fit her size-ten body into a size-four dress? Does she know the importance of persevering and refusing to give up? Have you taught her that sometimes sacrifice and service hurts? That at times we have to give up things we want to do in order to care for others?

Elisabeth Elliot's missionary service cost her a husband (he was killed by the Auca Indians he had gone to serve). Amy Carmichael shunned the fashionable dress of her day and began donning the clothes of the East Indians she was determined to reach with the gospel. Such women represent true heroism and faith, something that never goes out of style.

Some years ago, I befriended a man who worked at the gas station where I regularly filled my tank. He and his wife had little kids, and they hit some hard times. When I learned about his story, I went home and told our family about it.

"They're going to have a tight Christmas," I said. "How can we help them?"

When I let the kids come to their own conclusion, somebody came up with the idea that they could donate some of their own toys for Christmas gifts. I made a point of reminding them that for something to really be a gift, they would need to consider giving away toys they really enjoyed, not just toys they never played with and knew that another child wouldn't either.

Holly wasn't into stuffed animals that much, but there were two she did treasure. One was a stuffed wolf named Lilac; the other was a raccoon with Olympic circles on it, which Holly had gotten for her birthday just a few weeks before.

I remember watching Holly suddenly clutch that raccoon with a new intensity. "It's really cool, Dad," she said. Finally, she handed it over. "You said we should give the best that we can—and raccoon and Lilac are my best."

Let your daughters know it's okay to hurt a little bit while serving. Christ willingly went to the cross, but you never see Him depicted on that instrument of torture with a smile on His face.

Aware of the need to teach this truth to my daughters, I ultimately went to Colson's benefit, though I admit I tucked a mini-television under my coat. When I wasn't on the stage, I got to see the action on the court—as well as those lucky saps who were sitting in my seats!

I tried to look like I was paying attention to every word Chuck was saying. My little two-inch television (with the sound turned off) was cradled in my hands in such a position that it looked like I was sitting at the table with my hands clasped. But you can't fool Colson, the lawyer.

Apparently, he noticed the television's reflections off my eyeglasses. Speaking at the podium, he broke stride and asked, "What's the score, Kevin?"

Everybody laughed, and I, the baby of the family, was thoroughly embarrassed.

My daughters loved this story, and it was helpful for them to hear that it hurt a little bit for me to do what was right in this situation. They knew I wanted to go to that game more than just about anything else. In fact, it is not overly dramatic to say that for those two-and a-half hours, there was nowhere else on earth I would rather have been than courtside at the Final Four tournament.

But I missed it.

Learning to put others first does more than add integrity to our daughters' walk with God. It also helps ensure that they will have rewarding marriages, as putting your spouse first is crucial to marital satisfaction.

Real Love

One of the burdens of being a Leman is having to listen to your dad lecture. Not at home, mind you, but often at school. Holly attended a great little Presbyterian school, Grove City College in Grove City, Pennsylvania, and the school officials there asked me to talk for two hours on everything the kids needed to know about sex.

I checked with Holly first. Imagine listening to your father—with everybody knowing he's your father—as he stands in front of your peers, talking about a weenie, a tallywhacker, or the thing, not to mention "little big man." But Holly gave me the go-ahead, so I showed up, hoping to impart some helpful knowledge while also not tempting my daughter to disown me.

"Guys, I want you to listen for a moment," I encouraged them near the end of the talk. "Put ten years on your life and pretend you're married. You're in the rack with your spouse"—I paused, and at this point, the males invariably did their war whoop, an odd mixture of Tarzan's call and the school fight song—"and you're sleeping." *Groans. Boos.* Apparently, *in bed* and *sleeping* are not synonyms for these kids.)

"All of a sudden you hear this loud, ratchety noise. You wake up in a fog and reach for the phone, but that's not where the sound is coming from. Then you reach for the radio, but it's not from there, either. Next, you realize that croaking sound is coming from the chest and throat of your sweetheart. She's sicker than a dog.

"'Honey, you've gotta help me,' she says, so you lead her toward the bathroom, but halfway there she throws a four-and-a-half-footer onto the floor. She's blowing more chunks than you've ever seen in your life."

The kids were howling. "Oooooh! Grooooosss!"

"Guess who's gonna clean that up?" I asked them, and suddenly there was a dead silence.

Fast-forward several years. Holly was back east with her fiancé's family. They weren't married yet, so they were sleeping in separate rooms when Holly heard a loud hacking and coughing. She got up to see what was wrong, and there was her sweetheart, having a midnight meditative session with the toilet bowl.

He occasionally missed too.

"Daddy, I'm so glad I sat through your lectures," Holly told me. "I spent the night cleaning up vomit."

Holly realized that in that one four-hour stretch with her fiancé she had learned far more about the reality of marital love than she did watching all the Sandra Bullock, Tom Cruise, Julia Roberts, and Richard Gere movies combined.

I've realized that I can make my daughters' lives go much more smoothly by helping them to see that for most of us, life serves up ten helpings of reality for every one helping of bliss. Marriage is about service even more than it is about romance.

This is true even when it comes to sex and conversation. Men, we're going to address that most difficult of all subjects, how to talk to your daughter about sex. It's our responsibility to clue our daughters in to how a man wants to be served this way in marriage (just as we must teach our sons how to serve their wives in this same area). Your daughter won't "intuit" a true understanding of male desire on her own; we can help our daughters by addressing exactly how a wife can put her husband first in this regard.

I mentioned earlier in this book that men seek sexual *fulfillment*, not just sex. I'm willing to bet that many wives would, indeed, put sex at the top of their list when asked what is most important to their husbands. But sex without sexual fulfillment to a man is like conversing with a man through a newspaper is to a woman. The woman does all the talking, the man occasionally says "huh?" and the wife gets the distinct impression that hubby is simply going through the motions and doesn't have a clue what she is really saying. She might seek conversation, but not when it's like *that*.

Ask that same woman what the difference between sex and sexual fulfillment is, and she's likely to shake her head. Sexual fulfillment is not when the wife says, "Okay, if you really think you need to, I'll try not to pretend I'm tired and the house is a mess, but could we hurry up and get it over with? That way I can get back up and finish cleaning the kitchen."

Sexual fulfillment is not based on a wife's *willingness* but rather on a wife's *eagerness*. It's very kind of a wife to be willing, but having her become merely a willing receptacle is not fulfilling to the man. Sure, as guys we'll take sex any way we can get it, but we'd much rather have it come from an eager participant.

I know I'm preaching to the choir here, but I have yet to meet a man who doesn't occasionally want his wife to initiate sexual relations. If we want our daughters and their husbands to enjoy this basic aspect of marriage, we can help prepare them. Sadly, I've had far too many women tell me in counseling, "My mom pulled me aside on my wedding day and said, 'Sex is something you're going to have to learn to live with. Just lie back and let him enjoy himself; it usually doesn't take all that long if you just let him get it over with.'"

What a crippling thing to say! Instead of talking to our daughters this way, we can tell them, "Rather than always assenting, try asking! If you really want your husband to reach the gloried heights of fulfilling sex, surprise him! Let him see you in something he's never seen you in before. The mere thought that you *planned* this, without him asking you to, will rock his world. Set up new experiences, tell him over and over how important, how vital this aspect of marriage is to you, and then back that up with actions."

If any women are reading this chapter, I know they'll be saying to themselves, "I'll never get there. Sex will never be that exciting to me." That's *exactly* why I'm encouraging fathers to teach their daughters to put other people first. It's rather elementary. Do you think your daughter has an emotional (as well as financial and spiritual) stake in her husband's marital contentment? Do you think she ultimately wants her hubby to drive to work saying to himself, "I'm so glad I married that woman"?

Of course she does! And you can help her achieve that goal by showing her what makes a man glad he married a woman. Don't make her go through three husbands to find this out—help her get it right the first time. She needs to know that sex may never be as important to her as it is to her husband, but she can still initiate it because her *husband's love and affection* are important to her.

Lest someone think I believe only women must serve, let me stress that I tell men to put the same principles into play. If this were a book about mothers and sons, I'd start talking about how important it is for mothers to tell their young men how crucial it is to put the newspaper down when their wives want to talk. It's just as crucial for men to put others first as it is for women. And marriage provides plenty of opportunities for men to do this.

For instance, I've yet to meet a man who could honestly answer most of the personal ads you see in the newspaper: "Single female, in search of caring, understanding male, who enjoys long walks, quiet meditative talks, cuddling by the fire, and watching romantic comedies." Give me a break! Husbands generally don't come home from work saying, "I can't wait to sit down and have a forty-five minute talk with my wife." But I urge men to do it just the same, because it matters to their wives.

Most of the couples who come into my office suffer from the same disease: selfishness. They place their marriage in a Catch-22: The wife refuses to initiate more sexually because the husband doesn't care a hangnail about romance. The husband says it's too hard to think romantically if he doesn't get enough sex. Unless both husband and wife take the initiative, such marriages will devolve into bitter accusa-tion and unmet needs.

Daughters who have been taught that other people matter more have been given a great head start in marriage. They will find more ful-fillment outside the relationship, as they serve others, as well as inside the relationship, as they build intimacy with their spouse.

Putting other people first has limits, of course. There are times when service can be crippling rather than enabling, and we need to teach our daughters that too.

"Dad, Why Won't You Help Him?"

When Holly was still young enough to always hold my hand as we walked together, we passed an older man with white hair and a cane sit-ting on a bench. There's no charitable way to put this, but it was obvi-ous to me that the man was drunk. I steered Holly away from him when he called out, "Excuse me, sir, can you help me?"

I squeezed Holly's hand and gently said, "Come on, honey, let's get out of here."

"But, Dad, he asked for our help," Holly protested.

"We can't help him, Holly," I tried to explain. "He just wants money, and money isn't what he needs."

Holly was just six or seven years old. As the firstborn, however, she has always seen things in black or white, and she couldn't accept me walking by a man who asked for help.

"I thought you said we should help others. That's what Jesus would do."

"We should, Holly, but giving that man money won't help him. It will hurt him."

We went to a grocery store to pick out some food, but Holly wouldn't give it a rest. Every other minute, she came back to me with, "I still think it's terrible that we didn't help him."

About a half hour had passed, so I finally said, "All right, Holly, I'll tell you what I'm gonna do. We're going to go back to that man, and I'll show you why we can't help him."

We went back and, not surprisingly, the man was sprawled out on his back, mumbling and drunk as a skunk, passed out on the sidewalk.

"What happened?" Holly asked.

"Somebody gave him some money, and he bought the bottle you see him holding in his hand. If we had given him money, that's what he would have spent it on."

Holly was strangely silent.

"It *is* important to help people," I added, "but sometimes, the best thing you can do is pray for someone and not give them money."

I want to raise daughters who know the meaning of sacrificial service, but I draw a distinction between sacrificial service and enabling people to destroy themselves. For instance, I don't recommend that a woman stay with a man who is physically abusing her just because she needs to "put him first." That's not what I'm talking about. What a controlling, abusive man needs more than anything else is someone who will stand up to him and say, "Not any more."

That's true service.

Section Three
Daddy's Dilemmas

CHAPTER 12
When Mother and Daughter Collide (and Daddy Is in the Middle)

Typical scenario: Baby is one week old and she wakes up crying in the middle of the night. The wife is so exhausted that for the first time since the baby was born she manages to stay asleep.

Hubby hears the crying and nudges his wife awake. "The baby is crying," he says. "She must be hungry."

The wife listens for a moment. "She's not hungry; she's just wet."

"How do you know?" the husband asks.

"Just *listen* to her cry. She's not hungry; she's wet. When she's hungry, her cry sounds different. *You* change her. I need the sleep."

Hubby is 98 percent skeptical here, but he's an empathetic man and wants to give his wife a break, so he gets up, changes baby's diaper, and, sure enough, baby falls back to sleep.

Mothers have an uncanny sense of what their babies need and an amazing, almost intuitive understanding of what their children are trying to communicate. Unfortunately, this can hold back a child's development. Mothers can become so adept at anticipating a child's desires, the child may not learn how to communicate those needs effectively.

According to researchers, this is just one of the ways that an active father can help his daughter develop. When a father interacts with his baby, the child is forced to learn how to communicate more effectively. Dad's supposed weakness in this regard is in reality strength.

This is just one of many examples of how crucial a father is in all stages of a daughter's life. Until relatively recently, in terms of Western culture, no one questioned the importance of fathering. It might surprise some of you men to learn that in colonial America, fathers were viewed as the primary caregivers to children. Until the earlier part of the eighteenth century, virtually all child-rearing manuals were written for men. And it wasn't until the nineteenth century that women began to be awarded custody of children in the wake of a divorce. Prior to that, children almost always went to the man.[1]

But today, for good or for ill, child-rearing has become, in the popular mind at least, the domain of mothers more than fathers. While many women's groups bemoan this fact and sometimes insinuate that most men are just neglectful slobs, in many homes moms don't *want* dads' involvement—at least not with their children. Contrary to popular belief, there is a growing body of evidence which suggests that "only a minority of women seems to desire increased participation by their husbands in child care, and that the rates are not appreciably higher for employed than for non-employed mothers."[2] Many women, in fact, actively discourage their husbands from taking paternal leave. When asked, some of these women admitted that they did not want to risk the child's bonding with the father, thereby competing with their own bonding process.

This is a dilemma that needs to be addressed. Men, if you are married to one of these mothers, you need to be firm. Your daughter needs your involvement. Some of you may have wives who consciously or unconsciously sabotage father-daughter intimacy out of a sense of competition, a fear of losing power, or a perceived threat to their own identity. Unfortunately, a few mothers think fathers should bring in the bucks and leave child-rearing to them. If daddies start parenting, some mothers worry that they will no longer have any exclusive role. Thus their own sense of inadequacy deprives their daughters.

The research shows that a mother's attitude toward the father-daughter relationship has a major impact on a father's parental involvement. If the husband perceives that his wife doesn't want him to be influential in his daughter's life, or if the wife makes the husband feel as if he knows nothing about being a female and should therefore leave matters of substance to her, hubby is far less likely to become the active, affirming father that his daughter craves.

Another way that mothers can unwittingly (or wittingly) sabotage father-daughter relations is by insisting that a father parent like a mother. When a dad becomes involved in his daughter's life, he will bring his own opinions, values, and beliefs to the relationship. He may seem brusque where the mother would be gentle. You cannot expect a man to parent like a woman. The ideal is *not* for a child to have two mommies, but for a child to have a mommy *and* a daddy.

It is my experience that men married to women who view a father's participation with a latent hostility are too willing to "go along" for the sake of peace. They might try to take steps forward, but ultimately they give up and hold back. I want you dads to understand just how vital your care and participation in the parenting process is so this doesn't happen in your home.

A Man for All Seasons

Just as a father's attention is vital to help a baby learn to communicate, so it is essential just a few months later as the near-toddler learns to accept a man's attention. Dr. James Herzog points out that both boys and girls have an acute need to identify with their male parent, particularly between the ages of fourteen and seventeen months, which results in them gravitating toward Daddy.[3] Insecure mothers may feel jealous or even betrayed by this—*I changed her diapers, I'm the one who helped her take her first step, I rocked her to sleep and dressed her in clean clothes, and now she wants him more than me?!* —but this is a necessary development that mothers should encourage, not hinder.

Dr. Charles Flatter points out that as toddlers become children, a father's need to become actively involved increases yet again. Little four-year-old girls learn that Mother and Daddy resolve conflicts in different ways. One parent might be more analytical; the other more emotional. Whatever the case, the daughter will learn that there is more than one way to handle a dispute. If the father draws back, the daughter will be one-dimensional and much less able to cope in a varied world.

Competition can heat up fast. It is normal for a five-year-old girl to begin to flirt with her father and even be resentful of her mother. Her longing for the father's affection at this age is such that she envies the exclusive relationship Mommy has with Daddy. This, again, is a crucial step that helps the little girl define her femininity, regardless of how painful it might be for Mom.

Between the ages of six and preadolescence, a daughter's view of Daddy will transform itself from an idealized one to a more objective characterization. Dr. Phyllis Tyson has found that an involved father at this season of life helps a daughter learn to manage her impulses and cement her gender identity. Also important, an involved father will help a child this age to begin the necessary separation from the mother, stemming the natural urge, caused by fear, to regress to being a "baby" again.[4]

The potential for conflict here is obvious. The child *needs* to separate from Mom if she is going to become an adult, and she will naturally use Daddy to help make that transition. Mother might take this personally and blame the father for a natural process of life.

In adolescence, the involved father becomes the male figure that all other men are compared to. His acceptance, affirmation, and encouragement will help the daughter successfully negotiate her way into adulthood. I'm all for the mother and daughter being "best friends" at this age, but mother shouldn't guard this so possessively that daughter is cheated from receiving Dad's all-important attention. Dad, you need to step forward here and stay involved.

In every stage of life—from birth to marriage—an active father's presence is crucial. Unfortunately, the father's role in each case can seem threatening to the mother: "He doesn't know how to handle a baby!" "She's *flirting* with him, treating me like an outsider! And I'm her own mother!" "Why must he insist that Annie grow up? So what if she wants to be my baby again?"

Have you heard any of these comments in your own home? Depending on a mother's own strength, these thoughts will either sow the seeds of dissension and conflict or be accepted as the natural course of a girl growing into a woman.

Men, if your wife is undermining your relationship with your daughter, ask her to read this chapter. Talk over her fears. Don't discount them, but don't simply give in to them, either. Listen to your wife, assure her of your love, but affirm your desire and intention to remain active in your daughter's life.

After you've done that, however, I want you to take another step and put the spotlight on yourself. Maybe your wife feels threatened by your parenting in part because you've been neglecting her in favor of your daughter. It's no more healthy for your daughter to have a man who is involved in her life but ignoring her mother than it is for her to have a father who ignores her. She needs to see a healthy marriage in order to develop an appropriate model for her own marriage.

Successful fathering stands on two pillars: being an active father and being an active husband. Let's now turn our attention to this second element.

The Father As an Active, Involved Husband

Jim has two daughters and a gorgeous wife named Alice, who could easily be a model. When Alice walks into a restaurant, men's heads turn.

Jim is fun loving and affectionate—with his daughters. He treats them tenderly and lovingly and is very involved in their lives, showing up for their soccer games and ballet recitals and even making it to many of their practices.

Nobody could fault him for his love as a dad.

When it comes to loving Alice, however, Jim has some room to grow. Alice has a clear love language: "I need to be touched; I need to be caressed; I need to be catered to; I need to be talked to." In other words, Alice wants to be pursued like Jim pursues his daughters, but Jim almost never touches his wife. He shows surprisingly little interest in her, sexual or otherwise.

Talking with Jim and Alice, I discovered that Jim grew up in a strict home. Kids were expected to obey without question and speak only when spoken to. Jim can't recall even one instance in which he witnessed his father kissing his mother, holding her hand, or affectionately hugging her.

Intellectually, Jim knows he shouldn't treat Alice like his father treated his mother. Though Jim is fully aware of how cruelly treated his wife feels when he remains so distant, he still seems incapable of pursuing her.

Alice is understandably perplexed. Many a man has made a snide remark or even an overt advance—and she has spurned every one. But her husband—whom she would love to show interest in her—treats her like a copy of last week's classified ads.

Men, I've never met a wife who told me, "I'm so thankful that I'm number two in my husband's heart and his children are number one."

Our job as men is to move toward our wives.

Going on the Offense

Even when we're tired. Even when we're under job stress. Even when we've been talking all day and feel like we've run out of words, we need to move toward our wives. You may have a jerk boss who rides you unmercifully and unfairly. But when you allow him to send you home in a funk, you let that man afflict your wife and children too. It's your job to protect your family from that jerk.

Parenting your daughter is obviously very important to you, since you're reading this book. One of the ways you can serve your daughter is by loving your wife the way she wants to be loved. Women don't feel loved when they sense their husband is controlling—and control is often our number one failing as men. I've found that a number of men sometimes aren't even aware that what they are doing could be considered "controlling" behavior, so let me be very specific here.

Janice comes home after spending an hour and a half shopping for groceries and is met at the door by meticulous Mark. Mark actually requests the receipt, then does an itemized accounting of everything Janice bought. "Why did you buy this newfangled Go-gurt for the kids instead of regular yogurt? You know it's more expensive."

"I just thought they'd like a special treat for after school, that's all."

"And what's this ten bucks for gourmet coffee?"

"I'm having some friends over and didn't want to serve them Folgers."

"I thought we were going to start conserving . . ."

This type of control mongering is debilitating to a woman.

Other men use their temper to exert control. They know that as soon as they start bellowing like a lion, their wives and kids will quickly fall into line. When these men are tired, they don't even try to relate— they just yell.

Another type of controlling man (one that, I must confess, mystifies me!) is the husband who refrains from ever initiating sex. He's turned the stereotypical tables around and uses sex as a tool of manipulation rather than of delight. Typically this occurs only when the husband knows the wife desires more sexual activity. Rather than smile and enjoy it, as many men would do, this man maliciously withholds his affection and makes his wife suffer.

You may not realize what you're doing. On the other hand, some of you may be completely aware of the game you're playing. What even these latter men may not realize, however, is that they are inflicting damage not just on their wives but also on their daughters.

If you go along with a subpar marriage, your daughter will pay the price. She needs to have a strong, involved, affectionate, and respectful marriage modeled for her. The best gift you can give your daughter is making your wife number one in your eyes. You are not raising healthy children if you shower all your attention on "Daddy's little girl" and leave nothing for Daddy's wife.

Building on a strong marriage, both father and mother can give their children something priceless—cooperating parents.

Cooperating Parents

Max and fifteen-year-old Beth were out for a drive one day when Beth started talking about college. Beth is the type of daughter who is very reserved and talks only when she wants to; even then, it is always on her terms (typically, this occurs when she and her dad are in the car or doing something else so that they don't have to sit eye to eye). Consequently, Max has learned to listen carefully when Beth is in the mood to relate.

Max accepted this and made himself available. As Beth expressed her confusion over where she wanted to go to school, Max finally asked her, "Well, honey, what do you want to do after college?"

Beth paused, then admitted, "I don't know. I only know what I *don't* want to do."

"And what's that?"

"Work."

Max couldn't help himself; the belly laugh was spontaneous. "You know, Bethie, working is part of this world."

"I know that. I'm willing to work, but I want to work like Mom—at home. I want to be a mom."

Max then said something rather insightful. "If you want to be like Mom, then you better marry someone like Dad, someone who is committed to the values of having the mother stay at home and raise the kids. Not every man will want that."

What Max did was make the husband-wife relationship complementary to the father-daughter relationship. He wanted Beth to see that he and his wife work together as a unit. If Beth wants the life her mother enjoys, she'll need to pick a husband who is similar to her father.

Think of how comforting this is to a girl. She has both a good father and a good mother modeled to her. Together, they help her to understand how a man and a woman relate, work together, and raise a healthy family. There are no holes for her to fill in, no gaps to reconstruct. She has the entire package right before her—how a godly woman lives, how a godly man behaves, and how both of them relate to each other.

Isn't this what you want for your daughter, Dad? Don't you want her to have the best chance for happiness in her own marriage? If so, learn to get along with your wife. Shower your daughter with affection, but save the primary flow of your attention for your wife. If you do this, your daughter will benefit all the more.

CHAPTER 13
When Daughter Develops

It's ten o'clock on a Sunday night. Sande calls out, "Honnnneeey?"

This is different from your normal "honey." "Honnnneeey" means she has an agenda.

"What?" I ask.

"Would you do me a big favor?"

"Like what?"

"Would you run down to Walgreen's for me?"

"Walgreen's? For what?"

"Well, I just started my . . ."

"Oh no, don't ask me to do that. Don't say that. Please. Anything but that. I'm not going. The answer is no."

Ten minutes later, I'm parking my car and walking into Walgreen's. Next thing I know, I'm standing in the feminine hygiene section, amazed that something so little can have so many different varieties. Not wanting to come back anytime soon, I buy a box of forty. "That ought to hold her for a while," I tell myself.

Do you think those tampons were right? Of course not. I still don't know exactly why (but Sande made it clear that they weren't the proper kind, strength, what have you). They specifically said they were super. A hint to the men: Don't be fooled by the word *super*. It's a trap. *Super* doesn't mean squat.

So ten minutes later, I'm going back to the store, only this time, I decide to take the shotgun approach.

I buy them all. Natural, unnatural, super modified wings, plastic, cardboard, regular, scented, unscented. There wasn't a style, label, or brand that didn't find its way into my cart. "Now all I have to do is get out of here," I said to myself.

Unfortunately, the way out had to be traveled through a nineteen-year-old clerk with four earrings in one ear and about three packs of gum in her mouth.

"So, you want these in a bag?" she asks, popping her gum.

"No," I say to myself. "Let's show the entire neighborhood how big a sap Kevin Leman is when it comes to buying feminine hygiene products."

Largely because of this experience, I'm willing to concede that there are some things only a mother and daughter should discuss—such as buying tampons. But sex is definitely *not* one of these things. It is a classic case of absolutely the worst timing when a father begins to pull back from his physically developing daughter. That is precisely the time that he should be drawing near. A father's love is a safe harbor for a developing young woman.

Sadly, I've read numerous studies conducted in the 1980s and 1990s confirming that a father's involvement with his daughter usually decreases as the daughter grows older. The nature of a father's interaction tends to change as well. One study found that fathers of adolescent daughters tend to restrict their involvement to their child's academic performance and future plans, not even touching on issues of her present daily life (boys, clothes, friends, recreation). These fathers are making themselves obsolete way too soon.

I can't tell you how many mothers have come up to me and lamented a conversation between themselves and their husbands that goes something like this:

"Well, Marge, little Susie is, uh, well, you know, developing."

"Developing?" Marge asks coyly.

"Yeah, she's uh, well, she's getting, I mean..."

"*Breasts*, Harvey. They're called breasts. She's fourteen years old. That's perfectly normal."

"Well, maybe you oughta have a talk with her or something."

What hurts even more is when Marge notices that dad is a little more reluctant to hug his Susie.

At precisely the time that a young woman is cast into insecurity by a changing body, at exactly the moment when she is wondering how males will view her as a woman instead of as a child, father draws back. It will confirm all her worst fears and may even send her reeling into the arms of a hormone-driven boy who will gladly pay attention to her—for a very high price.

A good father will keep moving toward his developing daughter, and he'll be prepared to talk to her about modesty, which has become a lost virtue.

A Return to Modesty

Twenty-three-year-old Wendy Shalit, a gutsy Williams College student, rocked the literary world early in 1999 when she published her first book, *A Return to Modesty: Discovering the Lost Virtue.*

In this book Shalit takes on conventional wisdom and argues that many of the problems faced by today's young women are caused by the fact that they have lost respect for the neglected virtue of modesty. According to Shalit, promiscuity—often touted as women's emancipation—has not helped females but hindered them, resulting in low self-esteem for women and disrespect from men.

But this is the discovery that really challenged me. Quoting Joan Jacobs Brumberg's study of girls' diaries in *The Body Project*, Shalit recounts the following typical New Year's resolutions for a young woman living in the 1890s:

"Resolved, to think before speaking. To work seriously. To be self-restrained in conversations and actions. Not to let my thoughts wander. To be dignified. Interest myself more in others."

In the 1990s, the typical diary reads, "I will try to make myself better in any way I possibly can. . . . I will lose weight, get new lenses, already got new haircut, good makeup, new clothes, and accessories."[1]

Our culture has become so unbalanced, we may have to look outside our generation to find suitable role models for our daughters. Instead of raising girls whose highest dreams are to appear on the cover of the *Sports Illustrated* swimsuit issue (or worse), we can intrigue them with biographies of Amy Carmichael, Elisabeth Elliot, Clara Barton, or Elizabeth Dole.

And a good father will be prepared to talk to his daughter about sex because he's been talking about it since she was very young.

Cowardly He-Man

As a Navy Seal, there are few things Robert fears in this life. If you put him in hand-to-hand combat with just about anyone, Robert would come out on top. He's familiar with guns, and there isn't a model that's been invented that Robert would be afraid to shoot. He can walk along the side of a cliff with a three-hundred-foot drop and speak as casually as if he were taking a stroll through the park.

He's the type of guy who really doesn't need to use antiperspirant because he almost never sweats . . . except when it comes to his daughter's burgeoning sexuality.

How does a four-year-old girl do what opposing armies cannot?

Dads, don't fear your daughter's sexuality. God made them sexual. Your job is not to run from that but to channel it in the proper direction. In doing this, you will help ensure that your daughter is able to enjoy a very precious part of marriage.

When one of my daughters was quite young, we had some friends over. My daughter was watching television and started touching herself. Within a few minutes she was doing a pretty good bump and grind—at age three! Her Baptist mother was just about going into apoplexy trying to get my attention. "You're the psychologist! Do something!"

I got out of my chair, casually walked over to my daughter, and picked her up. "Honey," I said, "listen. You know, touching yourself like that—well, we all touch ourselves—but if you really want to touch yourself like that, you should do it in the bedroom. Do you want to go up to your bedroom?"

"No, I want to watch TV!"

She didn't fully realize what she was doing. We looked at her actions through forty-something eyes. Through the experience of a three-year-old, her actions were virtually subconscious, more of a reflex than an active interest.

Notice, I didn't make a big deal about it. Neither did I ignore it.

Above all, don't be afraid. Passivity in this area has wounded so many little girls. Talk about sex. Give your daughters a safe environment to learn about this mystery, and provide them with a biblical context that will keep them out of a lot of trouble.

Safe Sex

I'm not suggesting this is necessarily *easy* for me, but if I don't talk to my daughter about sex, you know who will? A hormone-raging teenager who has designs on my daughter, that's who. Or an amoral editor of the latest teen magazine who commissions articles on premarital sexuality. It would be abnormal for any adolescent daughter not to be at least a little curious about sex. Of course she is going to seek answers. If a daughter senses that her dad is not willing to discuss these things with her, she's going to go somewhere else to pursue her answers, and you'll have absolutely no control over what she hears.

That thought scares me even more than the thought of talking about sex with my daughters. If you have to use one fear to conquer another, go ahead—as long as you get over your silence. Talking about sex is not a mother's job. It's a dad's job. A young girl deserves to hear about sex in a safe environment from a man she trusts—her father.

Don't misunderstand me—your daughter may very well say the *last* thing she wants to hear spoken from your mouth are the words *sex* or, especially, *penis*. When my daughters were younger, it wasn't unusual for them to say, "Dad, I don't really want to be hearing this." We didn't have a one-time sex talk. We had many regular talks that came up in the normal course of life, so they had plenty of opportunities to pretend they didn't want to discuss the more private aspects of being a human being.

Though my oldest two daughters sometimes seemed to shun my words, they eventually grew up and told me, "Dad, even though we said out loud, 'We don't want to hear this,' inside we were saying, 'Thanks, Dad, we really do need to know this.'"

I can hear some of you asking, "But what do I say, Leman?"

Let me go through a short discussion I've had with my own children:

"Dad, don't you think sex is gross?" one daughter asked me.

"Let me ask you a question, honey. Can you trust Daddy?"

"Yeah."

"Has Daddy ever lied to you?"

"No."

"Okay. What I'm about to say to you is the truth." What I'm doing here is cashing in on the safe relationship I have with my daughter. Sex seems scary when you're young, but because my daughter and I have a trusting relationship, my daughter will be less fearful when she enters that world with my guidance.

"This won't sound like the truth to you right now. You're too young. But the day is going to come when the thought of having sex with a man—with your husband—is going to sound very good to you. I know it's hard to believe, but the day will come.

"God is the creator of sex. Sex is not something dirty; it's very wonderful within marriage between a husband and a wife. The world out there makes it nasty. There's pornography and other things that demean women, but the way God originally designed it, sex is a very precious experience between two people who are committed to each other for the rest of their lives."

I then do something I think is crucial. I introduce sex in its spiritual context. Sex is not about pleasure; primarily, it's about two people becoming one. I emphasize this because I want sex outside of marriage to sound as absurd as it is.

"The Bible tells us in Genesis 2 that the two—the husband and wife—will become one. Now, how can two people become one? You know math, right? One plus one doesn't usually equal one, does it? Sex is one of the ways that two people come together emotionally, physically, and spiritually."

I've been through this enough times that I know my daughter will ask me questions at this point. "Why does everybody talk about it so much?" is a common one.

"Well, honey, sex feels very good. Have you ever noticed how some parts of your body feel very nice when they are touched? Doesn't it feel special to get a back rub from Mom or Dad?"

"Yeah."

"Well, sex is like that, only more so."

Now, doesn't this sound like a much healthier introduction for a little girl into the world of sexuality? She's talking to a man whom she trusts and who will never violate that trust. She's hearing about it in a biblical context, and she's being imprinted to remember that sex is something reserved for marriage.

Every little girl deserves no less, and only her father can give that to her. Don't rely on a junior high teacher. Dad, don't expect your pastor, youth group leader, or physician to do what you should do. Especially don't let your daughter's sexual education come through the sex-hungry mind of a teenage boy.

Let it come from you.

Another practical tip I've learned—particularly with pubescents—is that the best place to talk about sex is in the car. That way, both father and daughter can look out the window while they're talking. It can be a bit intimidating to sit across from each other and peer into your little girl's eyes while you mention body parts.

Just as difficult as talking about sex, however (though every bit as important), is modeling a healthy sex life.

You're Still Doing It?

My wife and I were taking two of our daughters through a book that helped to explain some of the facts of life. The illustrations were chastely drawn, but made it quite clear that the mommy and daddy weren't wearing clothes underneath the covers.

"That's so gross," one of my daughters protested.

"What is, honey?" Sande asked.

"Being naked under the covers."

"Well, how do you think you got here?" I asked her.

Suddenly, a light went on in my precious daughter's head. At first, there was this glimmer of understanding in her eyes, which was quickly overcome by the fires of sheer indignation.

"You mean you and Mommy get naked under the covers?"

"Yes, we do," I said.

This was followed by a Sherlock Holmes *Aha!* "So *that's* why you lock your door on Saturday mornings! And I thought you just wanted to be nice to us when you let us watch cartoons!"

"Uh-oh, honey," Sande smiled. "You've blown our cover."

Actually, it was amazing our cover had lasted as long as it did. When Kevin and Krissy were very little, I frequently shushed them downstairs, told them to watch whatever they wanted, and explained that Mommy and Daddy really needed to "talk."

They left, I bolted the door in four places, and got under the covers with Sande. Within minutes, Kevin and Krissy were back at the door.

"Daddy? Daddy? Are you in there? We can't hear you talking. I thought you said you and Mommy needed to talk."

"Get away from that door!" I yelled. It was the tone only a father can use, and it worked to great effect. (Yelling is actually one of my spiritual gifts, second only to beeping the horn.) I heard those tiny feet scamper away faster than if they'd seen a monster.

But little kids have short attention spans, and at what had to be absolutely the worst timing of their lives, Krissy and Kevin knocked on the door once again. Unfortunately, by this time I'm living on another planet. The only world that exists is beneath me, and I can't even remember whether I have children, much less what their names are. So, great psychologist that I am, I plead with Sande, "Let's not say anything, and maybe they'll go away."

Sande looks at me like, "I sacrificed for thirteen years past college to get you through your doctorate, and you come up with *this?!*"

Finally, we hear Krissy say to her brother, "Kevey, looks like you better go get the hammer. I think they may need our help."

With those words I come crashing back into Earth's atmosphere. Incidents such as these help to explain why many an audience has heard me mutter, "We have seen the enemy and they are small—and unionized."

While very young kids can make intimacy difficult, a daughter deserves a father who is crazy about his wife. A daughter also needs a mother who welcomes her husband's advances. When a husband comes home from work and comes up behind his wife for a little innocent grope and she says, "Harold, not now! The children will see!" My response is, "What better thing for a child to see than a father who is eager to touch his wife and a mother who is eager to receive that touch?"

I don't apologize for liking sex. I think God's creativity hit a grand slam on that one. So it's not a stretch for me to say that I want my daughters to enjoy that same experience, provided it's within marriage. Which makes it my responsibility to model a healthy and affirming attitude toward sexuality.

Of course, this has to be done appropriately. Some friends of mine are rather on the heavy side, and during one interlude—somewhere between ecstasy and bliss—they managed to fall out of bed. The man's arm hit a side table and knocked a lamp over, creating such a ruckus their two teenaged kids rushed into the room, thinking some major catastrophe must have taken place.

Much to their horror, there were Mother and Father in all their glory, rolling on the floor and reaching furiously for some covers.

Interestingly enough, the kids weren't uptight about what their parents were doing—though no parent should intentionally provide such a blatant reminder. They were more upset that their parents had forgotten to lock the door.

During the mid-1990s, Cathi Woods directed a tremendously effective abstinence program for teens in Rhea County, Tennessee. She discovered something that I think is tremendously sad. Woods says, "I'm surprised at the number [of teens] who say, 'My parents don't have sex, no way.'"

Cathi has found one exception to this group—kids of single parents. "These kids know their parents are having sex because they see the partner staying over," Woods adds.

What kind of society are we building when kids with married parents think sex never takes place, but kids with single parents know it takes place? In too many kids' minds, sex has become virtually synonymous with sin.

"Kids think sex is dirty," Woods told *Christianity Today*, "but it's not. They're just experiencing it in the wrong context. The reason they think of it as dirty is because girls feel dirty and used after the fact. The two comments I hear most often from sexually active young girls are, 'I feel dirty' and 'I feel used.'"[2]

What I want to do for my daughters is to model a healthy, sin-free sexuality that will build up a woman and unite her with her husband—the way God intended. That means I have to go out of my way to talk about sex with older children, using very relevant terms.

Telling the Truth

I believe it is important to communicate frankly with kids about sex and to talk to them on their level. I followed that policy with my own kids, and I practice it when I talk to youth groups or classes in schools.

One of my favorite talks is titled "Help! I've Got a Rocket in My Pocket!" This title might shock some of you, but I've found that it is crucial to be at ease with the subject in order to get through to young people. I just try to get them to see the ridiculousness of how most of their peers behave.

"Tell me," I'll ask a class. "What's so pleasurable about grabbing a girl's boob when she walks by you in the hall? What is it? Are you some kind of freak that you actually enjoy that? Half the time it hurts when they slap you. Quite frankly, you need to know how to caress a boob if you want it to feel good. Just reaching out and grabbing somebody without their permission, however, isn't cool—it's sexual harassment."

The kids laugh, and I'm creating an environment that opens them up to be challenged. In their minds, I'm an "old" married man, but I still enjoy sex—*with my wife*. I'll get nowhere if I tell them, "Sex really isn't that big of a deal. It's overrated." I've heard pastors actually try this approach; kids just snicker and think the "old man" has absolutely nothing to say to them, because in their minds, sex is everything.

I want to be honest. Sex is a precious thing—in the right context.

I made that very clear to my son. "Why don't you be different, Kevin? Why don't you be the one guy girls know won't pinch their bottoms or call out a number when they walk by? See if you can't rise above the Neanderthals who masquerade as men."

That's a challenge to be mature. The reason we can't be afraid to use understandable language is because in today's world, kids need specifics. A girl needs to know that it doesn't take much to make a fourteen-year-old boy—or a twenty-four-year-old boy, for that matter—get sexually excited. She also needs to be forewarned that a sexually excited boy tends to get more aggressive than a girl would expect, and that the vast majority of those aggressive boys will keep being aggressive until they are told, quite firmly, to stop.

You can't speak in generalities here. I'm very specific.

"You know, honey, if you sit in a boy's lap, he feels sexually stimulated."

"No! Are you serious? Just sitting in his lap?"

"That's right. That's all it takes."

I also tell my girls about the importance of dressing modestly, but I put this in a positive light. "If you ask most mature men what they like best—a woman who is smartly dressed or a woman who is scantily dressed—most of them will say, 'I like the one who is smartly dressed. It's nice to have something left to the imagination.'"

"It takes little creativity to dress in a scanty fashion; it takes practice and good sense to learn how to dress smartly. You need to start practicing now."

Instead of taking away my daughter's "fun," I'm adding to it, encouraging her to consider creating a bit of intrigue rather than blatant immodesty.

This is all part of leading my daughters to "still waters."

Still Waters

Psalm 23:2 provides a great model for parents: "He leads me beside the still waters."

I grew up near the Niagara River in upstate New York—there was *nothing* still about that river. It was a churning, frothing whirlpool.

You can't make wise decisions in a churning, frothing whirlpool. You're just trying to keep your head above water and trying to avoid drowning. That's why a good shepherd cares for his sheep by leading them to *still* waters, where they can think and rest and be slowly nurtured to health.

It finally hit me one day: *This "still waters" concept is why you don't let your kids go hang out at the mall.* The mall does not constitute "still waters." The mall is full of temptations. The mall is a churning, frothing allure, and some kids will be pulled away by the floodwater.

As my daughters grow physically, it's my duty as their shepherd to provide them with still waters. I know how hormones can rage if a young woman and a young man see an R-rated movie, go to a dance and start touching, and then hang out for two hours in a parked car. It doesn't take a psychiatrist to figure out what's going to come off in that backseat, so I'm not going to let my daughter get into that situation.

Instead, I'll help her create an appropriate alternative. "Sure, honey, you can spend time with Robert. Bring him over and we'll all watch *The Three Amigos* together!" If she doesn't want to watch a video, we'll play a card game, go for a walk, or any number of things—provided it's done in a context where my daughter is not threatened by floodwater.

I can imagine what some of you are saying: "Isn't that sheltering your daughter a little too much, Leman? When are you going to let her grow up?"

I didn't hold my kids hands down on a lit stove to show them the stove was hot. I taught them about heat and then guided them away from the coils. When our girls were really young, we plugged the electrical outlets so they wouldn't be tempted to electrocute themselves. Now they're old enough to handle electricity and stoves without getting into trouble.

In the same way, I'm not going to throw my daughter into a sexual environment and hope she finds her way. She may be sixteen years old, but she hasn't been dealing with sixteen-year-old boys for more than a few months; in that respect, she's still a baby and needs to be protected. I don't teach my daughter about sexuality by letting her take her shirt off in the backseat of a car when she's sitting next to an anxious adolescent boy. She doesn't need to be in that situation.

Of course, once the sixteen-year-old becomes nineteen and then twenty-one, things change dramatically. As my two oldest daughters reached adulthood, both of them entered relationships that made Sande and me uncomfortable. But what do you do when a twenty-four-year-old daughter has her heart set on a young man? You can offer advice, but at that age, she's old enough to make marital choices on her own. It would definitely be inappropriate for us to isolate or even direct the dating habits of a twenty-four-year-old daughter. But I believe it would be just as inappropriate to treat a sixteen-year-old girl like a twenty-four-year-old woman.

Fortunately, our two oldest daughters have now made choices we're very pleased with. I like to think that they had enough time in the soothing environment of still waters to learn how to make wise decisions for themselves.

Men, I can't be too strong here. The statistics for premarital sex are appalling. If you have more than one daughter, odds are that at least one of them will be sexually active before marriage—and very likely end up pregnant. If you do nothing, if you ignore the whole issue and hope it just goes away, odds are that *every one* of your daughters will become sexually active before marriage.

If you talk to crisis pregnancy center directors like Cathi Woods, you'll find that the vast majority of these young women live with tremendous regret. Most of them will say—as Cathi says of herself—"If God would grant me just one wish, I would wish that I could be a virgin on my wedding night."

Don't let your daughter learn through neglect and regret. This is an area where pain is too severe. If your daughter becomes sexually active, she risks venereal diseases, a broken heart, intimacy problems in marriage, and more. It's too risky not to take shepherding in this area very, very seriously.

On the other hand, an involved, affirming, and open father can steer his daughter around promiscuity. He can walk three or four different virgin daughters down the aisle to marry their husbands. The privilege of doing this, however, won't happen by accident. Dad will need to be heavily involved in his daughters' lives.

He'll also need to model chastity by being faithful to his own wife.

Doorway to Promiscuity

Kelly was just fourteen years old when her mother was horrified to learn she had left the following message on a boy's answering machine: "Let's have S-E-X." When confronted, Kelly was far from contrite. On the contrary, she insisted she was determined to lose her virginity within the next twelve months. "I want it to be now," she told Amy Bach, who writes for the *Arizona Republic*.[3]

Marylyn McEwen teaches public-health nursing at the University of Arizona. A number of years ago, she was shocked to discover a note in the pocket of her fourteen-year-old son's jeans. The girl who wrote the letter was whining because she and McEwen's son hadn't had sex even though "we've been going out for two to three weeks now."

Promiscuity among young girls has reached such a point that Ann Landers received the following letter: "In the old days, mothers warned their daughters about boys who were out for all they could get. Today, it's the boys who need protection."

Health and sex education teacher Lyle Kelly told the *Arizona*

Republic that teenage girls often admit to him that they don't enjoy sex but that they do it for emotional comfort.[4] If a girl is getting this emotional comfort from a dad who lives with her and is involved in her life, she will not need to seek it from a lust-riddled boyfriend.

Dr. Lisa Gabardi's studies back this up. Gabardi examined the differences in regard to sexual activity between college students from divorced families and from intact families. Her conclusions weren't surprising. Students from divorced families had more sexual partners and desired more sexual involvement when going steady than did students from intact families. In fact, parental marital conflict was a significant predictor of total number of sexual partners.[5]

This means that not only is it important for parents to stay together, but it is also important that they learn to stay together peaceably and lovingly, avoiding emotional as well as legal divorce.

I'm afraid I might start sounding like a broken record, but once again, the dad's first duty is to provide a safe environment in which both mother and father are present. If you do this, many of the other problems can be addressed. If you fail in this, you will face an uphill battle for the rest of your daughter's life.

CHAPTER 14
Father-in-Law

I never saw it coming. Sande sensed that something was up, but I didn't have a clue.

It was the middle of October 1998. I was watching the University of Arizona football team engage in battle with Washington's Huskies.

At halftime, Arizona was winning, and I was in a good mood. Apparently, Krissy's suitor—Dennis O'Reilly—noticed this and decided then would be as good a time as any to let me know he was going to take my daughter away.

For life.

I walked into the kitchen and was stopped short when Dennis asked, "Could I speak to you a second?"

There was a tone in his voice that tipped me off. He wasn't about to ask me how work was going at the office. I knew we weren't going to discuss the merits of the latest Buick over the newest Ford. This was something *much* more serious, and the only serious thing Dennis and I had in common was Krissy.

Suddenly, the Leman females poured out of that kitchen as if someone had just announced a plague. My radar isn't that dim. I knew *something* was going on.

"Sure," I said.

He got right to it.

"I'd like to have Krissy's hand in marriage."

A slow smile crossed my face. "You know," I said, "I could make this very difficult for you . . . or real easy."

I saw him swallow. His Adam's apple took down a lump the size of Mount Everest.

"I sure hope you make it easy," he said.

I could tell that the girls were in the next room, listening through the door. If I had quickly pulled it open, they would have all fallen into the kitchen. This was the most public "private" conversation I'd ever had.

I decided to make it easy, welcomed Dennis into the family, and gave him a big hug.

And then the girls had to come back in and pretend they didn't know what had happened!

One of the difficult things about seeing a daughter get married is that a dad tends to remember how little *he* knew when he tied the knot—and that scares him to death when he realizes his daughter is now on the receiving end of that ignorance.

When I asked Sande to marry me, I did so many things wrong it's a wonder we ever got together. First of all, no one ever told me to take her to a nice restaurant to propose. I took her to a field out behind my parents' house.

And then I put the ring on the wrong hand.

When we went down to city hall, I told Sande it was a Leman tradition for the bride to pay for the wedding license.

"Oh, how interesting," she said. "I certainly don't want to break a Leman family tradition."

It was only after she coughed up the five dollars that I had to admit she had just *started* the tradition.

I have to confess, I was so full of what was going on, so exhilarated by the thought that this beautiful young woman was willing to live with Cubby Leman for the rest of her life, that it never occurred to me what her father was thinking. I guess I assumed he was overflowing with unadulterated joy, but now that I've switched generations, I know exactly what her dad was thinking: *A stranger is taking my daughter away!*

As fathers, we are naturally protective of daughters. I think of my girls getting married as a chapter that is closing, even though Sande insists it's the reverse—that an entirely new book is opening up for them.

"Just think," Sande boasts. "They'll invite us over to dinner. I won't have to cook so often!"

"Yeah, but can Krissy cook?"

"Well, no, but I'll teach her."

When I thought about Krissy feeding this son-in-law, I started to get nervous. She can pour a mean bowl of cereal, but I wasn't too confident about her making anything that required an oven.

Fortunately, she chose the right man. During Dennis's bachelor party, I watched with interest as he ordered a salad and the waitress asked him what kind of dressing he wanted on it.

"Oh, how about a little bit of everything?" he said.

If that's his approach—mixing French, Italian, and Thousand Island—he'll do just fine with whatever Krissy places in front of him.

Krissy has told me she "survived" her first meal. She cooked chicken and rice, and couldn't stop laughing over the fact that somebody was actually eating something she cooked.

Suddenly, Krissy started showing a new interest in recipes. I heard her ask Sande, "What does it mean to mince? What is the difference between *folding* something and *stirring* it?"

In all of this, my attitude was, *Hands off. She'll make it, just like her mom did.*

By the time a young man asks for your daughter's hand in marriage, most of your parenting will be done. The wet cement will have hardened into an indelible mold.

It's Already Done

Your daughter's ability to trust, her openness to sexual intimacy, and her overall imprinting are, for the most part, already determined. At this point, there's not a lot more you can do. I know that being hands off goes against your nature as man, but that's a much better approach than to suddenly try to fix everything that is wrong with your daughter or future son-in-law. It's crucial for fathers to understand that you can't use a six-month engagement to repair twenty-five years of neglect. If you try, you'll only make matters worse.

A good father-in-law is marked in part by what he *doesn't* do. Here, more than almost any other area of parenting, is where doing too much may be an even greater danger than doing too little.

I've learned, in just the short time I've been a father-in-law, not to take sides in a disagreement. Sande and I have memorized the words, "I'm sure you guys can handle it; I'm sure you'll work it out."

We used these phrases quite frequently when the kids quarreled, and we intend to keep right on using them when marital spats erupt. The beauty of these phrases is that they accomplish two ends: They keep you out of the argument while also giving a positive expectation: "Somehow, you guys will figure this out." That shows confidence in them *as a couple*.

One of the things we *can* do is help our daughters' husbands understand them better. During Dennis's bachelor party dinner, several people gave advice, and I was one of them. Knowing Krissy as I do, I reminded Dennis that Krissy craves quality time, so Dennis would have to be willing to give her that time.

There was a lot more I wanted to say, but I purposefully held back. I have resolved not to pry. If they buy a new car, I don't need to know if they've taken care of any debts first. That "stranger" needs the freedom to become a leader, and the last thing he needs is even the sense that his father-in-law is looking over his shoulder, waiting for him to make a mistake.

A radio listener gave me some of the best advice I've ever received in this regard: "Just shut up unless they ask you!" Sande and I have made a commitment to follow that listener's advice. Part of being a good father-in-law is keeping your nose in your own business!

This goes for holidays as well as every other aspect of life. As a father-in-law, I can't assume my kids will join us for traditional family get-togethers. Just after Krissy and Dennis were married, I casually mentioned to Dennis, "You two might have other plans, but would you like to join us for Easter brunch?"

"We'd love to," he said.

But for the first time in my life, I had to ask. Notice that I asked *Dennis*, not Krissy. And I have accepted the fact that sometime in the future, they will develop their own traditions and rituals. They're a couple now. I may soon hear, "We'd love to, but we're sorry. We've made other plans."

In fact, the time may come when I'll need to encourage them to *stay away* from our own family get-togethers. Rather than their coming to our house, we'll be going to theirs. For years I have taught couples the importance of creating their own family traditions. What's true for other kids is just as true for mine. I know we are entering a new era.

A New Era

One of the obstacles Dennis will have to overcome will be joining a family whose members have grown up in the pages of books and who have had their stories recounted in seminars all across the country. Excepting the current occupants of the White House, there may not be a more public family in the entire United States!

Just weeks after Dennis and Krissy were married, a writer asked Dennis what it was like to have Dr. Kevin Leman for a father-in-law. His answer was interesting.

"Throughout the whole process, I sensed from him a great deal of trust, which I appreciate. He doesn't know me all that well yet, but he seems to trust me, and that means a lot to me. He really trusts that I will do right by his daughter."

I was very pleased when I heard this, as that is exactly the message I want to convey.

Making the transition from father to father-in-law may not be easy, but it's essential—and rewarding. A friend reminded me that the absolutely best thing about being a father-in-law is this: The next woman in my family to have a baby won't be Sande!

EPILOGUE:
The Awfully Long Aisle

March 27, 1999: Kleenex supplies dipped precipitously low in Tucson, Arizona, as Krissy Leman changed her name to Kristin Leman O'Reilly.

One of the worst parts about this whole marriage business occurred shortly after the engagement, when my daughter started talking about a honeymoon.

"Honeymoon?" I said. "Now wait just a minute. I agreed to the wedding. But what is that word—*honeymoon*? Is that like, you mean, you actually plan to go *away* together?"

My kids had great sport with this. "Let's talk about the wedding and make Daddy cry," they liked to say.

For weeks before the wedding, my daughter listened to various forms of music as she carefully chose a wedding processional. She finally chose a trumpet piece called "Trumpet Voluntary." I'd hear about two bars of that composition and just lose it.

The Leman family developed a new word: *Setback.*

Krissy showed me the wedding invitations. I cried.

"Setback," I explained.

"Setback," Krissy repeated, shaking her head.

Two weeks later: "Dad, what do you think of this dress?"

My eyes got misty.

"Setback?" Krissy asked.

"Setback," I admitted, blubbering.

"Dad, are you going to be all right?" Krissy asked me once.

"Honey," I said. "I have one goal—to get down that aisle. After that, you're on your own. I'll be dead to the world."

I couldn't exactly draw encouragement from my past. Back when Krissy graduated from high school, the principal thought it would be a nice touch to ask me to give the commencement address. "Oh, *Dr. Leman* is right here in town and his daughter is graduating. Maybe he'd be the best person to talk to the departing seniors!"

That just proves principals don't understand me any better today than they did when they kept suspending me forty years ago.

For starters, I had to do something that I've done maybe three times in my life—wear a tie. And then I prepared to deliver my fifteen-minute talk. (I've yet to meet a graduating senior who wished the commencement talk had gone on a little longer.) After about seven minutes, I got to the part where I said, "We're not here to celebrate your accomplishments, we're here to celebrate your *life* . . ."

Those were the last words anybody heard me say. I completely lost it. After spending thirty to forty-five seconds (a very long time when you're in front of a large group of people) trying to compose myself and keep the blubbering to an acceptable degree, I finally waved and motioned, "That's it."

That is definitely the *last* time, for as long as I live, that I *ever* listen to a high school principal.

216

Wedding Week

For good reason, Krissy was genuinely concerned about my ability to perform one simple function—walk her down a hundred-foot-long rose-strewn aisle—so we started practicing at home. Suddenly my knees became oatmeal and my walk changed into that of a stroke victim. Krissy had to literally pull me along. Sometimes she even had to hold me up.

This presented some logistical problems. Krissy is a very trim young woman. I kissed scales good-bye years ago.

"Have you considered a side car?" I asked her. "Or a wheelchair? You know, maybe you could just push me down the aisle."

"Daddy," Krissy whined, "I'd really appreciate it if you could learn to do this upright."

Understandably concerned that her old man was going to make a spectacle of himself on the most important day of her life, Krissy resorted to some psychological tactics of her own.

"All right, Dad," she said one evening. "Tonight we're going to begin desensitizing you."

"Desensitizing me? What are you talking about?"

She pulled out a video: *Father of the Bride*. "You're gonna start watching this."

Father of the Bride is a Steve Martin comedy about a man surviving his daughter's wedding. I had seen it before and blubbered so much through it, I was wary of ever seeing it again.

"I don't know . . ." I said.

"Daaad," Krissy said forcefully, "*watch it!*"

I remembered some parts that were too close to home—like the scene where Steve Martin realizes the wedding planner is determined to transfer 80 percent of Steve Martin's life savings into his own bank account. Already I had been informed that I would be charged $1.50 for every slice of cake that was handed out.

"A dollar-fifty?" I asked Sande. "You mean to tell me, some roly-poly ten-year-old boy decides to have six pieces of cake and I'm personally out $9.00? Is that what you're telling me?"

"Krissy only gets married once," Sande told me.

"I'm gonna bring a stun gun," I threatened. "Anybody gets near that cake, and *zap!*"

With Krissy looking over my shoulder, I took the videotape and put it in the VCR. As soon as the credits started rolling, I lost it.

"Major setback," I choked out.

"I really thought we'd get past the words," *Dr.* Krissy Leman diagnosed. "You're worse off than I thought."

I resorted to watching a far more familiar and comforting film. As you know by now, I have watched *The Three Amigos* so often I can run through every line in the film by memory. I don't know how many hours that Holly, Krissy, Kevin II, Hannah, Lauren, and I have endured Sande's disbelieving clicks while we laugh along with Steve Martin, Chevy Chase, and Martin Short.

There's a scene near the beginning where the villain, El Guapo, gets very upset at the people of Santa Poco. He calls out, "People of Santa Poco, you are no longer under my protection."

As a wedding gift for Krissy, I decided to put our movie memories to good use. I took down a cartoon that has been hanging on our refrigerator for almost a decade. It shows two parents walking behind a teenage boy. The parents have the boy on a six-foot leash, and the boy is complaining, "I just want a little more freedom."

The cartoon was frayed, but still in good enough shape for me to use.

It hurt taking it off the refrigerator. I put it in a box, and included a note with the words, "Krissy, people of Santa Poco, you are no longer under my protection . . . But, I will always be a part of you, and you will always be a part of me. All my love, Daddy."

Then Krissy caught me off guard with her own gift—a book written by father and daughter Bob and Brooke Carlisle. I've quoted from this slim volume—*Butterfly Kisses*—already.

On the front page, Krissy wrote:

> Dad, Just because I'm getting married doesn't mean that I don't need my dad. I have always felt so close to you. I love you <u>so</u> much! Please remember that I'll always be your little girl. <u>Always!</u> Thank you for all your love and guidance. You have made me who I am. <u>I love you</u>!
>
> Krissy
> (your favorite!)

The staff at *Parent Talk* radio put together a let's-help-Kevin-get-through-this-wedding program about a week before the wedding took place. I was overwhelmed as good friends like Steve Arterburn, Gary Smalley, Dr. Jim Dobson, Dr. Jay Passavant, and Chuck and Jenni Borselino called in with their encouraging comments. What really broke me up was when the last call came in. It was Krissy, and after that, I was done.

Big-time setback.

During the show, Sande said she needed to warn me about something. "You need to see this before the wedding day, because it's really going to break you up," she said.

Krissy and Dennis wrote out the traditional thank-you comments in the wedding bulletin, but at the end, both of them added an individual personal note. Dennis wrote one to his mom, and Krissy wrote the following to me:

"To my dad . . . From baby steps to walking me down the aisle, you have always held my hand, and you will always have my heart. I love you."

Rehearsal Reversal

Finally the wedding weekend arrived. Every day I could identify more closely with Steve Martin in *Father of the Bride*. I had hand cramps from writing out checks and forcefully let everyone know that if I saw so much as one swan waddling around my house, I'd shoot it on the spot.

To be fair, Sande did a good job of reining in a mother-of-the-bride's costly ambition. However, she managed to sneak in an elaborate ice carving that, as of this writing, I haven't received the bill for yet, but other than that, she practiced due restraint.

At the rehearsal, the two pastors—John Aker (a former monk and one of the best teachers I've ever heard, a brilliant man who also loves ceremony and symbolism) and Dave Rhodes (an ordained pastor who is also the principal at Krissy's and Dennis's school) presided.

They told us where to walk and what to do, pretty mundane stuff for most people, but not, unfortunately, for blubbering Cubby. Krissy and I had to practice walking down that aisle. *In the church!*

"Come on, Dad, you can do it!" Krissy said. "Piece of cake!"

The first time, we did it without music. John corrected my miscues. "No, Dr. Leman, start off with your *left* foot, that's right, stay together with Krissy."

The next time they added the music. They might just as well have shot me with a dozen arrows and told me to stand upright.

I saw Lauren, my youngest, as the flower girl walk down the aisle first; Hannah, our first "surprise" child, followed as a bridesmaid; Kevin II stood up front as a groomsman; and Holly, my oldest, as the maid of honor was the last to walk down the aisle before us.

My life—everything I value, treasure, and hold dear— was in that church. God was so present in His love and grace to me that if He had appeared in bodily form, I wouldn't have been surprised.

And there was my own bride of thirty-two years (in a row—that's the important part!), Sande, looking as radiant as ever. What more could a man want?

Earlier in the week, I had made a sign that I kept looking at when I was on the air with *Parent Talk*. Just thinking about the wedding made my emotions bubble up, so I wrote out, "I'm okay, I'm brave." Whenever I got overwhelmed, I took out that piece of paper and looked at it.

Krissy clenched my biceps, letting me know that reverie time was over. I needed to start walking. The trumpets pounded my heart unmercifully, and I took a step.

This is just practice, Leman, you can do this, I kept telling myself, but I've never felt weaker in all my life.

Suddenly I looked up front and started laughing. My family and friends had come prepared. They all held up large placards that read, "You're okay, you're brave."

All my life, I've been the strength of our family. My kids came to me when they were scared. The Huggy Hairy game worked because they knew the scary man was really their dad, and he would never let anyone hurt them.

But now, these kids, even six-year-old Lauren, were holding *me* up. It was the "rehearsal reversal." I suddenly realized that my family was my strength, and this mixture of feeling weak and strong at the same time was one of the most moving, profound experiences and emotions I've ever known. I realized right then that there is nothing in life— absolutely nothing—that can mean more to a man than investing the time in family and having that investment returned in just this way.

Tribute

After the rehearsal, we went out to dinner, then returned to our home for dessert. I got up and said, "This is a time for any of you to say anything you'd like to Krissy and Dennis. After all, this is the last day of their lives as singles."

There were numerous moving comments, but two highlights came from siblings. Holly spoke up and gave as touching a tribute as I've ever heard. From day one, Holly shepherded her younger sister through life. I can't count the number of pictures we have in which Holly's arm is around Krissy (I'm still not sure if that's because she cared so much about her sister or that she wanted to make sure that A, she ran her life, and that B, Krissy stayed in her place!). As a father, it was tremendously fulfilling to see my two girls show such obvious love and care, and that my second daughter would choose her oldest sister as her maid of honor.

The second tribute came from Dennis's brother Paul. It is natural and inevitable that a man will ceaselessly size up a future son-in-law. You can't help it. Your daughter means so much to you, it's hard to imagine anyone else caring for her so well and so deeply.

This sizing up is hard to do. You can look the young guy in the eyes. You can consider what he does for a living. You can listen to him talk and gently prod him about his values, beliefs, and upbringing. But sometimes, when you hear siblings talk, you get a window into a man's soul that you could never get anywhere else.

Paul started choking up almost as soon as he started talking. "I don't know how many of you know this," he said, "but when our dad died, Denny quit school and worked in a factory for four years to support our family."

In Paul's genuine tears of respect and appreciation, my own heart was warmed. *Krissy will be okay*, I said to myself.

Wedding Day

The morning of the wedding, I awoke and looked at the digital clock: it was 5:16, Krissy's birthday (May 16). I started to cry and wasn't able to go back to sleep.

We had to arrive at the church at two o'clock for a four o'clock wedding. I wore a very traditional black tux with a vest, just like the groomsmen, and was relieved to discover that my tuxedo wasn't six inches too short. It was also comforting to learn that Kevin II knew how to handle the buttons, ties, clasps, and other confusing aspects of formal wear. Wherever he learned this stuff, it wasn't from me.

After I was dressed, I walked into the church library, which had been transformed into the bride's dressing room. It was the first time I saw Krissy with her bridal gown on, and she looked gorgeous; this is not a proud father's hyperbole. I was struck by how my little girl looked so grown up, like a woman should look, rather than like the little kid of my memories. She literally radiated the beauty of a mature woman.

After the entire wedding party was ready, Pastor John ordered everybody out of the church sanctuary. Krissy and Dennis still hadn't seen each other, and John wanted to make this moment special. He dimmed the lights above the pews. If it's possible for a church to seem romantic, then this sanctuary did. John then told Dennis to stand up front (facing the altar) and had Krissy walk in the door.

As Krissy slowly approached her groom, John slipped out and led the parents back in so we could watch. This was the first time Dennis saw Krissy in her wedding gown—his beautiful bride *and my daughter*—and I saw that Dennis's eyes were full, as is a groom's right and privilege.

It was a sweet, endearing moment. After ten minutes, I needed some fresh air and stepped back outside. I returned to the church library, where Krissy followed shortly thereafter.

"I miss him already," she said, and I realized how deeply in love my daughter was.

The Ceremony

Finally, the wedding coordinator started lining us up. This was it.

As I prepared to walk down that aisle, which now looked like it was at least ten miles long, I caught myself touching a ring on my finger. Krissy gave it to me several years ago. She had given an earlier boyfriend a ring, and when the relationship went south and the ring was returned, she couldn't bring herself to sell it, so she brought it to me.

"I want you to have this," Krissy told me, and never have I seen such liquid love flow out of a child's eyes, "because I know you'll *always* love me."

She didn't have to explain the hurt. She didn't have to lay it out for me. Young love is full of disappointment, and as much as we hardened adults dismiss it, young love can hurt deeply. Krissy ran to me as her refuge. Young guys would come and go, but Daddy would *always* love her.

But now another young man, Dennis, was pledging to do the same. He wouldn't come and go. He was committing to love my daughter until God took him from this earth. In a very real sense, Krissy would need to *leave me* and *cleave* to Dennis. Our Christmas Eve sleepovers (an annual Leman event where the entire family would sleep in sleeping bags on the floor of our family room so we could get up en masse and attack the Christmas presents together—very early) would give way to this new couple's own traditions. I could no longer assume that Krissy would be free to join in the family fun.

I touched my ring, then stole a quick glance at my daughter's unadorned hand. The ring bearer had her ring, and it hit me like a sledgehammer that I'd probably never see my daughter's naked finger again. I remember when she was just a baby—a tiny, blubbering little baby—and I'd put my finger into her fist, and she wrapped those fingers around me. They were so small, so fragile.

And now Krissy has the hands of a woman. She's going to wear a woman's ring.

It's funny, the things that fill your mind when your world is being turned upside down.

The church was filled, and my heart swelled as "Canon in D" rang out, which was the music Krissy had chosen for her bridesmaids to walk in to.

Lauren stepped forward, unbelievably cute in her formal dress, methodically spewing rose petals along the carpet. Hannah was behind her with the other bridesmaids and then, finally, Holly walked down as the maid of honor. Once Holly stood in her place, "Canon in D" stopped, and "Trumpet Voluntary" started.

This was my cue.

One step after another. That's how I did it. I've never been so nervous in all my life. I've spoken to crowds numbering in the tens of

225

thousands. On the radio and television, I've performed live in front of millions of people. Yet here I was scheduled to walk a hundred feet, say six words on cue, and sit down, but suddenly the task seemed overwhelming.

The reason was simple, really. None of that other stuff mattered half as much as what was taking place inside this church in Tucson, Arizona. Nothing can compare in importance to a man giving away his daughter in marriage. This was one of the most significant things I would *ever* do in my entire life.

After what seemed an eternity, Krissy and I were standing in front of the church. Somehow, I had made it, and Pastor John spoke out, "Dearly beloved, we are here to celebrate . . ."

Finally, he asked, "Who giveth this woman to the tender care and love of Dennis?"

I was *supposed* to say, "We do, her mother and I," but this was a once-in-a-lifetime event, and I wasn't quite ready to do that.

"Wait a minute, Pastor John," I said. Heads turned. I was miked so everyone could hear me.

With the inflection of *The Three Amigos*, which Krissy couldn't miss, I said, "Excuuuussse me. Wait here, honey; I'll be right back."

Most people there knew this was one of my favorite quips so they knew something was coming.

I stepped forward and positioned myself so I could see both Dennis and Krissy. I then said to the groom, "Dennis, I have loved Krissy for twenty-five years. I can't imagine any man loving her as much as I do, but I know you love God and I know you love Krissy.

"Dennis, we have raised our daughter as a special gift from God, and we have treasured her. Before I give her to you, I need to be assured that you're going to receive her as this most special gift from God. Will you do that?"

Dennis gulped. "I will," he said.

I smiled. "That was the right answer, Dennis."

Some people might wonder why I didn't put Dennis through this drill in private. Yet I had never said this to him. When he'd asked for Krissy's hand, I'd just given my blessing. But more importantly I felt I was giving away my precious daughter, to whom I'd devoted my life for the last twenty-some years, in public. Dennis could also promise to treat her tenderly—in public!

That taken care of, I went back, interlocked my arm with Krissy's, and said, "Pastor John, you better ask me that question again."

"Who giveth this woman to the tender care and love of Dennis?"

"We do, her mother and I, with expectations for a great marriage for our Krissy and *our* Dennis."

At that point, I kissed Krissy, stepped back, and gave my daughter away.

"Whew," Pastor John said, "I didn't think he was ever gonna sit down!"

Once settled in my pew, I started sobbing. Something wonderful was being born that afternoon; I had no doubt about that. But something was dying as well. Amid the sweetness was a pain that I couldn't ignore.

Sande patted my shoulder from the side; my mom patted me from behind.

Forty-five minutes later, Pastor John introduced "Mr. and Mrs. Dennis O'Reilly."

Last Dance

The reception included a traditional first dance between the bride and the groom, but then it was my turn. For the father-bride dance, Krissy had picked out the song "My Father's Eyes," made popular by Amy Grant. It was a particularly meaningful song for us, as everyone has always said that Krissy got her long eyelashes and light brown eyes from me.

For me, this was the most intimate time of the entire marriage celebration. Enfolding my grown, beautiful daughter in my arms was, at that moment, the only place in the world I wanted to be. Speaking to large crowds, writing books, even going to the Final Four paled in comparison to this.

Both Krissy and I were crying, and laughing, and crying some more. "Hey, Krissy," I said, "these tears are tears of joy, because I love you so much. We've always had a special time together, haven't we? You've been such a wonderful daughter. I couldn't ask for a better daughter."

"And I'll always be your little girl," she answered back.

Holding her close, I whispered to her my hope that she would have the best marriage ever, and that she and Dennis would get to know each other well and share the ups and downs of life with grateful and faith-filled hearts.

Something happened in that moment. I had begun to let go ever since Krissy had announced her engagement, but this dance completed that task. I remembered the first time we left Krissy with a baby-sitter; a few years later, we let her spend an entire day at school. Next, there were the all-night stay-overs at Grandma's or a friend's house. Following that, there came the weeklong camps, and then, the more substantial partings of college. Every absence was a step to this road when Krissy would no longer be under my direct care.

I held Krissy tightly, but when the music stopped, I opened my arms and let her go.

A couple of hours later, Sande and I were the last ones to leave the country club, but little did I know that Krissy and I weren't done yet, not quite.

I Wanna Come Home

When Holly and Krissy were growing up in Tucson, young enough to still be running around in sleepers (pajamas with the feet attached), my mom and dad lived just four miles south of us. On many a night, one or both of our girls frequently slept over at their house. Whenever my parents stopped by for a visit, Sande and I inevitably heard, "Can I 'pend the night with Grandma?"

We usually said yes, but there was a ritual that occurred when Krissy stayed over. I'd drop her and Holly off at Mom's, make sure they had their blankets and stuffed animals, give them kisses and hugs, and drive away.

As soon as I pulled into our driveway, I'd hear the phone ring.

"Hello?" I said.

A little tiny voice—Krissy's—would eke out, "I wanna come home."

It was always Krissy, never Holly. Remember the time she didn't want to stay at college? That's my second-born. New experiences are not her forte.

So I guess I shouldn't have been all that surprised—though I was—when our phone rang at about 11:45 the night of the wedding.

I picked up the receiver and could hardly believe it when I heard Krissy's voice on the other line. It was no longer the tiny, tinny voice of a child; her voice carried the rich tones of a mature woman who is also a naturally gifted singer. Krissy was calling from the resort where she and Dennis were spending their first night together.

"Dad, before I go to sleep, I just want to thank you so much for the wedding and all you've done to make this such a great day."

Dennis got on the phone right afterward and said, "Dad, I just want you to know, this call wasn't my idea."

It wasn't hard to believe him.

After the call, I returned to my pillow with a full, contented sigh. Krissy didn't want to come home. She had found a new one.

The Aftermath

On Sunday, we all met at one o'clock for a celebratory brunch. Krissy and Dennis opened presents and then went to their home for the night.

On Monday, they needed a ride to the airport and asked me to take them.

"Oh, I can't," I said. "I'm sure I have a meeting or something."

Not a chance!

I was delighted to take them. Remembering Krissy's discomfort with being away, I pulled Dennis aside and said, "Dennis, here, put this number in your back pocket."

"What is it?"

"It's a toll-free number to our home. Not tonight, but maybe tomorrow, Krissy is probably gonna say, 'I want to call home.' This will save you a few bucks. Those hotels really rip you off with long-distance calls.

"By the way, this number is just between you and me, okay?"

"Got it, Dad."

I drove them to the airport, but five minutes away from the terminal, I decided to pull off the side of the road.

"Can I pray with you guys?" I asked.

I explained that the smartest thing I ever did was pulling off the side of the road as Sande and I made our way out of Tucson right after we were married (driving a 1960 Corvair that burned forty-five quarts of oil during the trip from Tucson to San Diego) and praying that God would bless our marriage.

They readily agreed, and we held hands. "God," I prayed with as much sincerity as I've ever prayed, "keep Krissy and Dennis close to you. Help them to thoroughly understand each other. Bless their lives and give them a rich, rich marriage together."

Time seemed to bend forward, as if I could almost see the future. "Krissy," I said, "some day you're going to be driving little Madison— your pet name for your invisible, someday child—to the airport. You can tell Madison and her husband that it's a Leman tradition to stop and pray and ask God to bless your marriage."

In minutes we were at the airport. I helped Dennis with the bags, gave each kid a hug, and told Dennis once again to take care of my daughter. I thought about handing him some money; it would have been so easy, but I decided against it.

Later that night, as I had predicted, Krissy told Dennis she wanted to call home.

"Let me dial it for you, honey," he said.

Sande answered, and after a short, pleasant greeting, Krissy asked, "Is Dad there?"

Of course I was touched that she asked for me so soon. If an operator listened in, she wouldn't have heard a particularly profound call. In many ways, Krissy just wanted to thank me again, tell me she was safe, and brag about Dennis.

"When we arrived, our room wasn't ready," she said, "then after a long wait they finally checked us into a tiny closet with two single beds.

"At first, Dennis said, 'At least we have a room. We can handle this.' But I told him, 'Honey, I'm already feeling claustrophobic.'

"Daddy, Dennis went right down to the front desk, and guess what? We're in a *junior suite!*"

But this simple call was enough to send me on another round of crying. Sande teased me about how this was so difficult for both Krissy and me, but I silenced her when I remarked, "Oh yeah? Just wait until Kevin II gets married. I can't wait to see momma bear and baby cub go through this."

Two nights later, after Sande and I had put Lauren and Hannah to bed, the house was quiet and life had seemingly returned to normal, though I knew deep in my spirit that it had been irrevocably altered.

"Well," I said out loud, "I survived. I got through it."

I was ready to pat myself on the back for going through one of the most tumultuous yet rich experiences I had ever known. Now I could relax. Finally I could put myself back together and recover.

Except for the fact that Sande leaned over my shoulder and whispered, "And to think we only have to do this four more times . . ."

Notes

Chapter 1: The Missing Ingredient

1. Cited by David Boldt, "We Knew It All Along," *Arizona Daily Star*, 2 April 1996, A1.

2. Kirk Johnson and Judith Springer Riddle, "Fathers Are Crucial to Girls' Emotional Growth," *Arizona Daily Star*, 13 February 1998.

3. Aimee Phan, "Drugs Tied to Trouble with Dad," *USA Today*, 31 August 1999, 4D.

4. Jill Leiber, "Father-in-law Knows Best," *USA Today*, 26 January 1999, C1.

5. Alan Ebert, "Fathers and Daughters," *Good Housekeeping*, June 1992.

6. "Rating Television's Images of Fatherhood," *Fatherhood and TV*, The National Fatherhood Initiative, March 1999.

7. Barbara Ehrenreich and Frances Pox Given, "Women and the Welfare State," in Irving Howe, ed., *Alternatives: Proposals for America from the Democratic Left* (New York: Pantheon, 1984), 41–60.

Chapter 2: That Man Matters

1. Michael Mignard, "Someone Saw You Yesterday, Dad!" *Today's Father*, vol. 4, no. 1, A4.
2. Gordon Forbes, "Workaholic Coach . . ." *USA Today*, 15 January 1999.
3. Bob Carlisle, *Butterfly Kisses* (Nashville: J. Countryman, 1997). Used by permission.
4. Dr. Kimberlyn Rachael Anne Leary, "The Daughter's Experience of Her Father During the Transition to Young Adulthood," doctoral dissertation for the University of Michigan, 1988.

Chapter 3: A New Meaning to the Family Bed

1. Rita Koselka with Carrie Shook, "Born to Rebel?" *Forbes*, 10 March 1997.

Chapter 4: Daddy Attention Deficit Disorder (DADD)

1. Barbara Goulter and Joan Minninger, *The Father-Daughter Dance* (New York: G.P. Putnam's Sons, 1993).
2. Walter Chan, "The Hysterical Spouse," *Medical Aspects of Human Sexuality*, September 1985, vol. 9, no. 9, 122–133.
3. Dr. Lennart Forsman, "Parent-child Gender Interaction in the Relation Between Retrospective Self-Reports on Parental Love and Current Self-esteem," *Scandinavian Journal of Psychology*, 1989, vol. 30, no. 4, 275–282.
4. Mark K. O'Neil and Patricia White, "Psychodynamic Group Treatment of Young Adult Bulimic Women," *Canadian Journal of Psychiatry*, March 1987, vol. 32, no. 2, 153–155.
5. Gail Sheehy, "Hillary's Choice," *Vanity Fair*, February 1999.
6. Ibid.

Chapter 5: A Good Dad

1. Health and Fitness News Service, "More Girls Play Sports," *Tucson Citizen*, 8 December 1992.
2. Ibid.
3. Scott Simonson, "Pooley Winner First Time Out," *Arizona Daily Star*, 24 February 1999.
4. Alan Ebert, "Fathers and Daughters."
5. *U.S. News and World Report*, 2 August 1999, 45.
6. Ibid.

Chapter 10: God Doesn't Want to Be First in Your Daughter's Life

1. Bob Carlisle, *Butterfly Kisses* (Nashville: J. Countryman, 1997). Used by permission.
2. Rita Koselka with Carrie Shook, "Born to Rebel? Or Born to Conserve," *Forbes*, 10 March 1977, 146ff.

Chapter 11: Teach Your Daughter That Other People Matter More

1. Alan Ebert, "Fathers and Daughters."

Chapter 12: When Mother and Daughter Collide (and Daddy Is in the Middle)

1. David Blankenhorn, "The Good Family Man," MN Children Youth and Families Consortium Electronic Clearinghouse, www.cyfc.umn.edu.
2. Ronald Pitzer, "Research on Father Involvement," MN Children Youth and Families Consortium Electronic Clearinghouse.

3. Dr. Herzog's, Flatter's, and Tyson's comments are from "The Father's Role," edited by Katherine Ross, in *Sesame Street Parents*.

4. Ibid.

Chapter 13: When Daughter Develops

1. Wendy Shalit, *A Return to Modesty* (New York: Free Press, 1999).

2. Gary Thomas, "Where True Love Waits," *Christianity Today*, 1 March 1999.

3. Amy Bach, "Girls Becoming Sexually Active at Younger Age," *Arizona Daily Star*, 31 December 1991.

4. Ibid.

5. Lisa Gabardi, "Differences Between College Students from Divorced and Intact Families: Intimate Relationships," Colorado State University Doctoral Dissertation, 1990.

About the Author

Dr. Kevin Leman is the founder of Couples of Promise and has written twenty books on marriage and family. His books include *The New Birth Order Book, Parent Talk, Bringing Up Kids Without Tearing Them Down, Sex Begins in the Kitchen,* and *Living in a Step-family Without Getting Stepped On.*

A master communicator, Dr. Leman is an internationally known psychologist and humorist and cohosts the television program *RealFAMILIES.* He is also a regular guest on national radio and television talk shows, including *Oprah; Live with Regis and Kathie Lee; Good Morning America; The View;* CBS's *The Early Show;* and the *Today Show.*

Dr. Leman and his wife, Sande, live in Tucson, Arizona. They have five children—Holly, Krissy, Hannah, Lauren, and Kevin.

For information about speaking engagements or seminars, please write or call:

Dr. Kevin Leman
7355 N. Oracle Road, Suite 205
Tucson, AZ 85704
Phone: (520) 797-3830
Fax: (520) 797-3809

Don't miss these other books by Dr. Kevin Leman

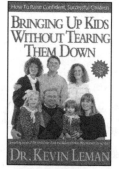

0-7852-7806-0
384 pages • *Paperback*

Kids who have a healthy self-image are kids who weather the storms of childhood and grow up to be confident, capable, and responsible adults. But too often, in an effort to build self-esteem in their children, parents actually accomplish the opposite. How is it that even with the best intentions, we can tear our kids down instead of building them up?

Bringing Up Kids Without Tearing Them Down is packed with tools you need to underwrite your kids' lives with a solid sense of self-worth and confidence. At the end of each chapter, you'll find steps to follow in your own family, plus self-evaluating questions that help you gain insight into your own parenting style. Also included is a question-and-answer section to help you quickly reference specific problem areas.

0-8407-3492-1
288 pages • *Hardcover*

What happens when you marry someone who has two children—one older than your firstborn son and one younger? Who is junior now? The firstborn? The middle child? *Living in a Step-Family Without Getting Stepped On* reveals that, as families are blended, shuffled, and rearranged, birth orders are anything but static. When children from two families are brought together by the marriage of their parents, all of them are plunged into what Dr. Leman calls the "birth order blender." Leman says, "The principles of this book will help you wage the battle of blending your family—and come out not only a survivor but also a winner!"

238

(Cont.)

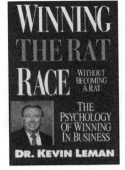

0-8407-3491-3
256 pages • *Hardcover*

The alarm clock that sounds off every morning signals your entrance into the rat race—the competition of life we all face, whether we like it or not. *Winning the Rat Race Without Becoming a Rat* takes you past the profit eye view of business success to the people eye view, giving you the relational skills necessary to reach your goals on both personal and professional levels.

You'll find information on how your birth order—and the birth order of your clients, customers, and employees—provides important keys for closing sales, establishing and maintaining contacts, developing corporate unity and productivity, and more. In addition to that, you'll learn to cultivate the unique strengths that come with your ranking in the birth-order scale–firstborn, later born, or only child—and gain insight into areas that may be hindering your growth and goal-setting.